Salim Durani

In a career spanning over 40 years, **Gulu Ezekiel** has reported and written on numerous sports from India and various parts of the world. His articles have featured in over 100 publications worldwide and he has appeared on numerous TV channels both as an anchor and guest expert. Gulu is the author of books on table tennis, the Olympics and cricket, including the bestselling biographies of Sachin Tendulkar, Sourav Ganguly and Mahendra Singh Dhoni. His books have been translated into multiple Indian languages. This is Gulu's fourth book for Rupa and seventeenth overall.

Salim Durani

The Prince of Indian Cricket

Gulu Ezekiel

Published by
Rupa Publications India Pvt. Ltd 2024
7/16, Ansari Road, Daryaganj
New Delhi 110002

Sales centres:
Bengaluru Chennai Hyderabad
Jaipur Kathmandu Kolkata
Mumbai Prayagraj

Copyright © Gulu Ezekiel 2024

The views and opinions expressed in this book are the author's own and the facts are as reported by him which have been verified to the extent possible, and the publishers are not in any way liable for the same.

While every effort has been made to trace copyright holders and obtain permission, this has not been possible in all cases; any omissions brought to our attention will be remedied in future editions.

All rights reserved.
No part of this publication may be reproduced, transmitted, or stored in a retrieval system, in any form or by any means, electronic, mechanical, photocopying, recording or otherwise, without the prior permission of the publisher.

P-ISBN: 978-93-6156-048-4
E-ISBN: 978-93-6156-782-7

First impression 2024

10 9 8 7 6 5 4 3 2 1

The moral right of the author has been asserted.

Printed in India

This book is sold subject to the condition that it shall not, by way of trade or otherwise, be lent, resold, hired out, or otherwise circulated, without the publisher's prior consent, in any form of binding or cover other than that in which it is published.

*To my beloved parents, Prof. Joe Ezekiel and
Mrs Khorshed Wadia Ezekiel, to whom I owe everything in life.
May their memories be a blessing.*

Contents

Foreword by Rajdeep Sardesai		ix
Introduction: Destiny's Child		xv
1.	Master Aziz	1
2.	Climbing the Ladder (1950–51 to 1959–60)	24
3.	Golden Run (1960–61 to 1964–65)	55
4.	Exile and Trauma (1965–66 to 1969–70)	89
5.	Back in the Fold (1970–71 to 1977–78)	117
6.	Life After Cricket	155
Acknowledgements		165
Appendix: Salim Durani Career Statistics (by Dharmender Chaudhary)		167
Index		173

Foreword

'*Kaise ho Rajdeep... Salim uncle bol raha hoon... Mai Dilli mein hoon...* (How are you Rajdeep... This is Salim uncle... I am in Delhi).'

It was an early morning phone call that woke me from my slumber in October 2020. The soft voice on the other line spoke with a distinct Kathiawari accent. Salim Durani, or Prince Salim to his many admirers, may have been born in Afghanistan or somewhere under the 'open skies' near the Khyber Pass while travelling on a camel caravan from Kabul to Karachi, but his heart was always in his beloved Jamnagar, the original home of cricket in Kathiawar or Saurashtra. I responded to Salim uncle's message promptly, 'Where are you staying uncle? I will come as soon as I can.' I hadn't seen Salim uncle or Salim bhai for a while. He was a cricket hero from my childhood years, a contemporary of my father Dilip Sardesai and his roommate on a historic tour of West Indies in 1971, a lingering connect with a past soaked in cricketing nostalgia.

Salim bhai was accompanied by Mahesh, his long-serving friend and Man Friday. 'We are here for a hospital inauguration of a friend in Vasant Kunj. Please join us,' informed Mahesh.

Not too many cricketers would be invited to be a guest of honour for a hospital inauguration in Vasant Kunj at the age of 86. But Salim bhai is a bit like Dev Anand—an eternal hero across generations—which is why even a much younger hospital entrepreneur was keen to have Durani as the chief guest.

Even those who had never seen him bat or bowl were mesmerized by stories of his all-round skills. Of how he had spun India to victory in consecutive Tests against Ted Dexter's England in 1961–62. How he had scored a century against the fearsome West Indian pace attack in the West Indies in 1962. How he was a crowd favourite who could hit a six almost on demand, leading to 'No Durani, no Test' placards at a stadium when he was dropped from a game in 1973. And yes, how he had taken the key wickets of Garry Sobers and Clive Lloyd to bowl India to a memorable first-ever win over West Indies at Port of Spain, Trinidad, in 1971.

As a Test player, Durani's statistics might not place him in the front row of great Indian cricketers. But the legend of Salim bhai was not born out of a number of centuries scored or five-wicket hauls taken. There are cricketers whose genius transcends the 22 yards of a pitch, whose contribution to the sport is defined by the manner in which they played the game.

Durani oozed charisma, an often indefinable *something* that makes certain people magnetic and attractive. He looked like a Hindi film star—indeed, he even acted once in a Hindi film—walked with a macho swagger and played sport with a carefree spirit that typified his debonair lifestyle. There was kindness in his heart and innocence in his soul. Cricket didn't bestow him with any of the riches that today's Indian Premier League (IPL) generation is blessed with, but he bore no grudges and never allowed the many bouncers that life threw at him to scar his character. He was often out of pocket but never far from laughter.

Which is why I didn't think twice before heading off to Vasant Kunj, finding my way through a maze of lanes before locating the place where Salim bhai was staying. '*Arre, Rajdeep tuh to papa Dilip jaisa hi dikhne laga hai* (You look just like your father Dilip),' he said, as we hugged each other warmly. He told me how he had not been keeping well during the pandemic but that his spirit remained undaunted. He still smoked several cigarettes every day, perhaps living up to his image as India's original Marlboro man equivalent. 'Most people in my family have lived into their nineties, so don't worry, I am also hoping to score a century!' he laughed.

We reminisced fondly about the 1971 West Indies tour; of how Salim bhai as my father's 'roomie' was in charge of making morning tea. 'I told Dilip that you have my *haath ki chai* and you will make a century. Sure enough he did. After that, my duty was to make the chai in the morning and his duty was to find a beachside place in the evening where we could get cheap beer!' he chuckled. We laughed a lot that afternoon, took a few pictures too. I guess I was a bit teary-eyed at the end of our conversation. My father had passed away in 2007. In Salim bhai's presence, I was reliving his memory too.

An hour later, as I was preparing to leave, Salim bhai, gracious as ever, asked me to come back the next day. 'Come in the evening, then we can enjoy a few drinks too!' he said with a wide smile. 'Don't worry, uncle. I will come and see you in Jamnagar soon,' I replied.

In November 2022, I was in Jamnagar for an election show. After the shoot had ended, I headed out to an address Salim bhai had given me. It was nightfall by the time we reached the place, only to be told that he was unwell and had been advised bed rest. Sadly, we couldn't meet. A few months later, I was on a morning walk when his friend, Mahesh, called to inform me that Salim bhai had passed away. I sighed and took a deep breath while feeling a sense of acute loss. Salim bhai had missed out on his life's century but he had left behind many wonderful memories. I could even picture him somewhere up in the skies with my late father, sipping their morning tea together before opening a beer can with infectious cheer. Just the thought was enough to bring a smile to the lips.

That night, I listened quietly to one of my favourite songs (also my caller tune) from the 1960s film *Hum Dono*: '*Main zindagi ka saath nibhata chala gaya, har fikr ko dhuen mein udata chala gaya!*' Dev Anand on the big screen, Salim Durani on the cricket field—evergreen heroes who lived life with a chutzpah that few have equalled.

Which is why exploring the life and times of Durani and his generation of cricketers is so valuable. Gulu Ezekiel, who is a devoted chronicler of the sport, is ideally suited to write a book like this. With his treasure trove of anecdotes, he brings the Durani era alive. It is only when we tell the stories of the past with passion that we can embrace the present. I am sure Salim bhai will appreciate the effort, as will every devoted Indian cricket fan.

Rajdeep Sardesai
Senior Journalist
Author of *Democracy's XI: The Great Indian Cricket Story*

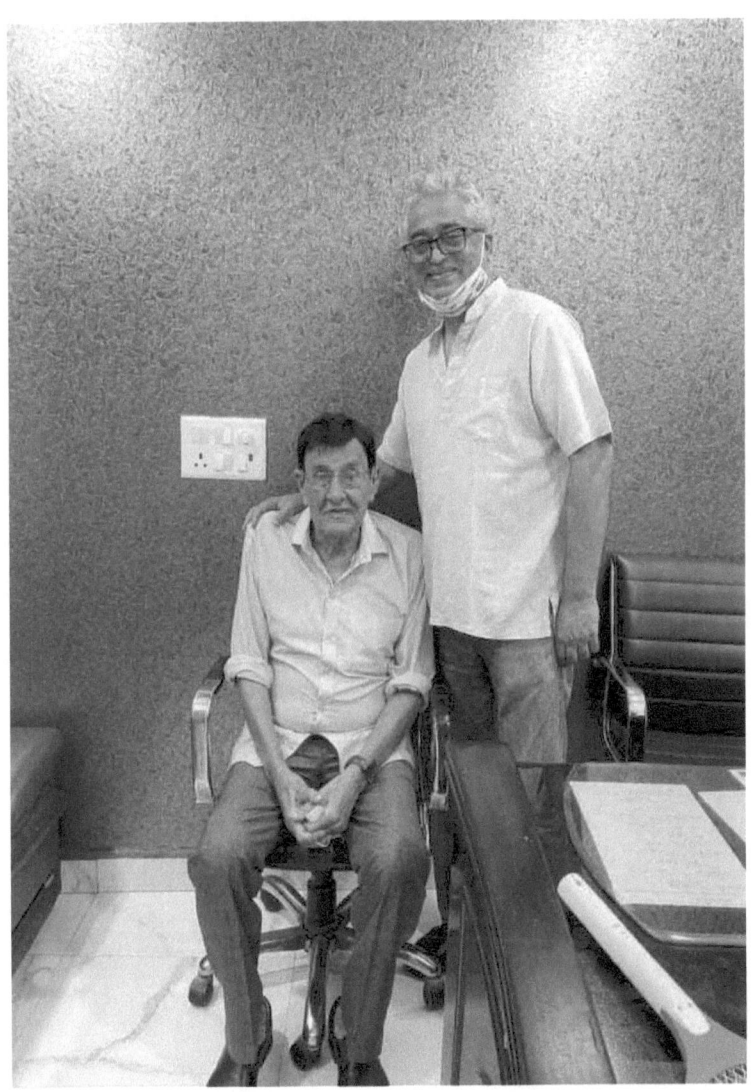
Photo courtesy: Rajdeep Sardesai

Introduction
Destiny's Child

To be a teenage cricket fan in 1970s Calcutta meant waiting with mounting anticipation for the times when the iconic Eden Gardens would host a Test match—an event that happened every two years. By the time the teams landed in the city, excitement would be at a fever pitch, accompanied by a mad scramble for tickets. In the days before televisions became a household feature—the internet was still decades away—the chance to get a glimpse of our heroes had us flocking not only to the stadium but also to the team hotel.

So, in late December 1974, on the eve of the third Test between India and West Indies, my school friend and I, along with hundreds of others, were camping on the pavement outside the Grand Hotel in Chowringhee, a short distance from Eden Gardens. The appearance of a tall, slim gentleman sent a ripple of excitement through the throng.

It was Salim Durani.

He was in town to watch the Test—he was then in his fortieth year, his international career over. Suddenly, all thoughts of waiting for the current Test stars disappeared as we rushed after him, autograph books in hand. The hotel security stopped us from entering but Durani patiently signed our books for a good 15 minutes before disappearing into the hotel to meet his mates. It was my introduction to his charisma and Pied Piper-like quality.

('Cricket's Pied Piper' was the headline for an editorial in *Indian Express* dated 4 April 2023. An editorial honouring a late sportsperson is unusual for a leading newspaper.)[1]

Like Victor Trumper, whom many Australian cricket followers place above the peerless Don Bradman, despite Trumper's statistics not being a patch on Bradman's, Durani's Test figures alone do not place him among the greats. But, like Trumper and many others in cricket history, his appeal and match-winning ability transcend mere numbers.

According to Ramachandra Guha, Durani—whom the former described as a 'wayward genius'—was the only Indian cricketer between Vinoo Mankad and Kapil Dev to win Test matches for India with both bat and ball.[2]

During his playing days, word would quickly spread when he was playing a match and crowds would flock to watch him bat. When he was dismissed, they would trickle out, disappointed that his time on the pitch was done. This was particularly so in Rajasthan, where he attained cult status.

Durani was a sixties icon. It was an era when India was beginning to register the odd Test victory—these included, for the first time ever, victories in matches played outside the country. But more than the wins it was the style and grace of a bunch of cricketers that caught the fancy of fans, young and old, male and female.

Durani—tall, lithe, light-eyed, with matinee-idol looks, whom journalist Suresh Menon memorably described as

---

[1] 'Express View: Salim Durani was Cricket's Pied Piper,' *The Indian Express*, 4 April 2023, http://tinyurl.com/4hbbuf26. Accessed on 13 February 2024.
[2] Guha, Ramachandra, *Wickets in the East: An Anecdotal History*, Oxford University Press, 1992, p. 145.

'irritatingly handsome and flamboyant'³—was joined by M.L. Jaisimha, Abbas Ali Baig, Mansur Ali Khan 'Tiger' Pataudi (the three representatives of Hyderabad, everyone's favourite neutral team) and dashing wicketkeepers Budhi Kunderan and Farokh Engineer in this elite group of style icons.

Jaisimha ('Jai') made the upturned collar and knotted white kerchief round the neck a style statement a decade before Australia's Ian Chappell arrived in India with his own collar style; Baig ('Buggy'), with his boyish good looks, was the first Indian sportsperson to be kissed on the field by an adoring female fan; Pataudi ('Tiger') had a naturally regal air about him—the fact that he could bat with panache even with only one good eye and that he was married to cinema's leading lady, Sharmila Tagore, made him a romantic favourite; Kunderan and Engineer batted with attacking flair—as did Durani—at a time when Indian cricket had unfortunately earned the tag of being the 'dull dogs' of international cricket. Legendary actor Dev Anand dubbed Durani and Kunderan 'the Gregory Peck and Sidney Poitier of Indian cricket'. Even back then in India, cricket and cinema shared a bond and this bunch were largely responsible for it. They not only had style but also had what one would today call *swag*, both on and off the field.

Durani was arguably the most enigmatic and most charismatic of his generation. His background and looks were considered 'exotic' by the masses, and his strokeplay was so dazzling he got the nickname 'Mr Sixer'. But that was only one of many epithets bestowed upon the man. He was also called 'Prince Salim', and with good reason.

Long before the phrase 'Bazball' was coined to describe the current England team's style of aggressive cricket, Durani played the game in the same positive manner in the 1960s and 1970s.

---

³Menon, Suresh, *Bishan: Portrait of a Cricketer*, Penguin India, New Delhi, 2011, p. 25.

He summed up his philosophy in an interview in 1979, 'Test matches are not won by planting both feet within the crease [...] I believed in going for my shots. I can defend thus far and no further. I've heard this criticism that I would've got more runs if I'd been more sober in my approach. Who's interested! I'm a creature of impulse. I go by my instinct. My instinct dictates my judgment. What joy is left in cricket if you play it like chess!'[4]

As I researched his life and career, I decided on another epithet—'Destiny's Child'. As you read his fascinating story, redolent with twists and turns and coincidences so uncanny they are hard to believe, you will understand why I gave him that sobriquet.

Following Durani's death on 2 April 2023, 50 years after his final Test match, there was a tremendous outpouring of emotional tributes from fans, friends, opponents and teammates, which was a major factor in my decision to write this book.

This is Prince Salim's story. Hang on for the ride.

Note: *I have gone with the original names of all cities—Madras (Chennai), Bombay (Mumbai), Calcutta (Kolkata), Bangalore (Bengaluru), Poona (Pune), and so on. In addition, I have used the terms 'Mysore State' for Karnataka and 'Madras State' for Tamil Nadu. This has been done because the events of the book are set in the period before they were renamed.*

All records mentioned pertain to men's cricket only.

In Salim Durani's time, the Indian cricket season would generally begin in September and continue till March or April of the subsequent year, i.e., September 1971–March/April 1972.

All England touring teams till 1976–1977 were known as MCC (Marylebone Cricket Club), but I have referred to them as England throughout the book.

---

[4]Bharatan, Raju, 'Wish They Had Let Me Hit Pak for Six!', *The Illustrated Weekly of India*, 25 November 1979.

One

Master Aziz

'Russia is a riddle wrapped in a mystery inside an enigma.' This famous quote from Winston Churchill could well be used to describe the birth, career and life of Salim Aziz Durani.

The first mystery surrounding Durani begins at his very birth. The major cricket databases attribute Kabul, Afghanistan, as his birthplace. This, despite my posting interviews over the years on X (formerly known as Twitter) tagging these databases, quoting Durani saying that he had never even been to Kabul let alone being born there.

Clayton Murzello wrote in *Mid-Day*, shortly after Durani's passing, 'Sports writer and historian Gulu Ezekiel has tried his best—especially over the last few days—to convince people that Durani wasn't born in Kabul.'[1]

The last major interview Durani gave, which appeared in *Sportstar* magazine, was to mark his eighty-sixth birthday on 11 December 2020. In it, he told G. Viswanath, 'I was not born in Kabul. In fact, I have never visited Kabul. My parents and *bade abba* [grandfather] belonged to Kabul. My bade abba was an automobile engineer. My grandfather played football in Kabul. The entire Durani family moved to Karachi in the

---

[1]Murzello, Clayton, 'Durani's Mumbai Connection Ran Deep', *Mid-Day*, 6 April 2023, http://tinyurl.com/45p7cxjz. Accessed on 7 April 2023.

second half of the 1930s. My father (Abdul Aziz) joined the police department there. He picked up cricket there and was a wicketkeeper-batsman. I don't remember much about Karachi.'[2] On the maternal side the family was in the dry fruits business.

In fact, years earlier, he had told Jaipur-based senior sports journalist Rameshwar Singh that the family moved from Karachi to Nawanagar (now Jamnagar)—an erstwhile princely state and now part of Gujarat—in 1935, when Salim was an infant.[3] In a text message to me, Rameshwar wrote, 'Salim-bhai told me that when the Durani family reached Jamnagar, they were received at the station by cricketers Vinoo Mankad, L. Amar Singh, his brother L. Ramji and Nariman Marshall. The Jam Sahib, Digvijaysinhji, gave them a quarter in Chaman Bhai ki Medhi where other cricketers lived. Vinoo took him from his mother's lap.'[4]

The other mystery surrounds Durani's date of birth. While 11 December 1934 is accepted as authentic, there were also mentions of 15 August 1938. But the latter has been proved false, as he was barely a year old when the family reached Jamnagar in 1935. Even the spelling of his surname has seen variations over the years—Durani/Durrani—though he always signed his name with a single 'R'.

So where then was Durani born if not in Kabul or even Karachi as has been mentioned on occasion? This is where his story takes an unusual turn.

---

[2] Viswanath, G., 'Salim Durani on His 86th Birthday: I Would Have Been Successful in ODIs, T20s', *Sportstar*, 11 December 2020, http://tinyurl.com/mtjk735v. Accessed on 13 February 2024.
[3] Saurashtra was a state from 1948 to 1956 of which Rajkot was the capital. It included Nawanagar (now Jamnagar). Though Saurashtra is not an independent state anymore and is now part of Gujarat, it continues to field a team in the Ranji Trophy.
[4] Text conversation with author, 8 April 2023.

Veteran Jaipur-based journalist Prakash Bhandari, who knew Durani for nearly 50 years, quoted him in an article written shortly after his passing, as stating, 'In cricket books, my place of birth is given as Kabul or Karachi, but I was born in some corner of the Khyber Pass under the open sky [...]'[5]

There is yet more evidence. Back in 2011, after receiving the Col C.K. Nayudu Lifetime Achievement Award from the Board of Control for Cricket in India (BCCI), R.C. Rajamani wrote in *The Hindu Businessline*, 'I asked the cricketer about two differing accounts of his birth...Kabul and Karachi. "Neither!" Pat came the puzzling answer. "I was born under the open skies in a caravan camp in the Khyber Pass... My mother and her younger brother were on their way from Kabul to Karachi... My mother developed labour pains as the caravan was crossing the historic site. It was weeks later when we reached Karachi, my birth was registered."'[6]

In quiz contests over the years, the question, 'How many Indian Test cricketers were born outside India?' is often asked. The standard answer has always been four: Lall Singh Gill (Rawang, Selangor, Federated Malay States, now Malaysia), Salim Durani (Kabul, Afghanistan), Ashok Gandotra (Rio de Janeiro, Brazil) and Rabindra 'Robin' Singh (Princes Town, Trinidad).

Quizzer, author and journalist Suvam Pal met Durani in Mumbai in 2015 during the shoot of a series on the history of Indian cricket called *Mid Wicket Tales* for the Epic Channel. Pal recounted in an article he wrote after Durani's death, 'Propagated by quizzers, trivia junkies and cricket experts, there is one myth about Salim Aziz Durani that perhaps first needs

---

[5] Bhandari, Prakash, 'I Would Have Been the King of Limited Overs Cricket', *rediff.com*, 7 April, 2023. http://tinyurl.com/f6zd59pv. Accessed on 17 April 2023.

[6] Rajamani, R.C., 'Bowled Over by Durani', *The Hindu Businessline*, 9 June 2011. http://tinyurl.com/2s4d25nv. Accessed on 6 April 2023.

to be broken. Durani, as it turns out, was not born in Kabul. I have heard this from the horse's mouth, from Durani himself [...] I was dying to ask: Was he really born in Kabul? Durani, a cricketer used to hitting sixes on demand, belted my query with characteristic nonchalance. "No, that's wrong. I was not born in Kabul. In fact, I have never visited Kabul, for that matter."'[7]

In fact, the Khyber Pass was then part of British India. Thus, the answer to the perennial question should be that three, and not four, Indian Test cricketers were born outside India. This does not include those born before 1947 in what would later become Pakistan and Bangladesh.[8]

Under the Open Skies

The phrase 'born under the open skies' appears to be a favourite of Durani's. Rameshwar says he first used the phrase in an interview for the Hindi daily *Rajasthan Patrika* in 2004.

Rameshwar, who as a child first saw Durani in action in 1966, describes in the 2004 interview how Durani joked that as his birth was 'under the open skies', it led him to 'always play my cricket with freedom'. He got to know Durani well both professionally and personally over a span of 30 years.

Of Pathan stock, Durani did have Afghan blood since both his father and paternal grandfather were born in Kabul. Thus, when the BCCI extended an invitation to him to attend the inaugural Afghanistan Test match against India in Bangalore in June 2018 as the first Afghanistan-born cricketer, Durani was happy to go along and enjoy the limelight one final time in

---

[7]Pal, Suvam, 'Salim Durani Had Satyajit Ray to Hemanta Mukherjee Impressed with His Chutzpah and Swag', *The Telegraph*, Kolkata, 3 April 2023, http://tinyurl.com/tpj3f6zk. Accessed on 10 April 2023.
[8]See also: Ezekiel, Gulu, *Myth-Busting: Indian Cricket behind the Headlines*, Rupa Publications, New Delhi, 2021, p. 186.

his star-studded life, according to Rameshwar. He was received warmly by the players and officials of both sides and had an emotional reunion with Sunil Gavaskar.

In the 'Special Portrait' section of the *Indian Cricket* annual for 1983, the late N.S. Ramaswami (NSR), who made a name for himself as a cricket writer in Madras, profiled Durani. But NSR was equally fascinated with history and in his write-up makes much of his subject's ethnicity.

'His proper name has some rather fierce historical associations [...] I do not know whether he has in his veins the blood of the Afghan tribe which once caused devastation in north India. If he has, it is no doubt a sign of the times that the right hand once raised in war and rapine plundered only opposing bowlers and destroyed only enemy batsmen [...] It is not a quibble to say that his right hand of war, in the old phrase, was his left hand. He batted left-handed and bowled left arm [...] If he is of Afghan Durani blood, he exhibited it in his batting, but with a difference. Like a warrior in the mountains of Afghanistan, he rushed at his enemy, the bowler, bat in hand (to speak metaphorically) not to wrest runs from him, but to charm them from him.'[9]

Along with his Afghan ancestry, cricket ran in his blood too. His father, Abdul Aziz, known as 'Master Aziz' in his coaching days in Pakistan, played one unofficial Test as a wicketkeeper against Jack Ryder's Australian team in Calcutta in 1935–36.

There is a revelation in the same 1983 *Indian Cricket* annual by the late Anandji Dossa, the doyen of Indian cricket statisticians: 'Salim's real surname is Khan. Durani is from the maternal side.'[10]

---

[9]Ramaswami, N.S., 'Special Portrait: Gifted All Rounder', *Indian Cricket* 1983, Kasturi & Sons Limited, Madras, 1983, p. 126.
[10]Ibid. Dossa, Anandji, p. 138.

The Durani blood that Ramaswami makes much of in his profile of Salim, therefore, appears to be from his mother's side.

'Khan' is a common surname among the Pathan tribe, the prime example being Pakistani legend Imran Khan. Suvam Pal quotes Durani saying that he had a cousin, Ain Rashid Khan, who was a senior police official in Calcutta, and obviously from his father's side of the family.[11] But herewith we shall refer to his father as Abdul Aziz and not Abdul Aziz Khan.

But why would Salim take his mother's surname? The probable answer to that will be revealed later in this chapter.

Before we proceed with his story, it is imperative we take a look at his father's life and career as well as the major part royalty played in the lives of both Salim and Aziz.

Aziz the Cricketer

Aziz first made his mark as a cricketer on the famed Roshanara Club ground in Delhi (the birthplace of the BCCI) in the 1930–31 season while representing Sind, of which Karachi is the capital, and where he was employed as a policeman. Aziz was born in 1905. Since Salim was born in 1934, when his mother was travelling from Kabul to Karachi with her younger brother, it appears that his father had already moved to Karachi, where his cricket career took off.

That season, Sind won the Delhi Tournament title. These matches are not listed in first-class records as they lasted only two days. Nonetheless, it was a prestigious event in North India back then in the years before the launch of the Ranji Trophy in 1934–35.

---

[11]Pal, Suvam, 'Salim Durani Had Satyajit Ray to Hemanta Mukherjee Impressed with His Chutzpah and Swag', *The Telegraph*, Kolkata, 3 April 2023. http://tinyurl.com/tpj3f6zk. Accessed on 10 April 2023.

Aziz was a wicketkeeper, a role his son briefly attempted before wisely giving up the big gloves. In the quarter-finals, Sind were up against the formidable Central India team, which was captained by none other than C.K. Nayudu who, just two years later, would become the first captain of India when it played against England at Lord's in 1932. They also had among their ranks two other players who would take part in that Lord's Test—wicketkeeper Janardan G. Navle and batsman Syed Wazir Ali. A fourth Lord's Test debutant was Aziz's teammate, the batsman and leg break bowler Naoomal Jeoomal.

In the event, Sind's crushing victory by an innings and 124 runs was a shocking result. On the first day, Central India were skittled out for just 127, Hyder Ali claiming five for 28 and Ahmed Botawala becoming the top scorer with 42 runs, followed by Nayudu's 19. Aziz took one catch, Wazir being the batsman and Hyder the bowler. By close of the first day, Sind had already taken the lead, ending on 191 for five with Minocher Mobed batting on 36 and MA Gopaldas on nine. Opener M.J. Abdullah had held the fort with 82 runs. Aziz fell lbw to Botawala for just one run at 174 for five.

The next day, Mobed, who would go on to represent the Parsis in the Pentangular tournament, completed his century, making Sind's total 346—a target much too high for their opponents. Batting the second time round, Central India were this time dismissed for 96, Nayudu (41) scoring the lion's share, and Hyder picking up his second five-wicket haul in the match.

Sind won their semi-final by an innings against Delhi, a team that boasted opener A.S. de Mello and Jack Brittain-Jones—two names that would go on to become notable ones in Indian cricket history. Aziz did not bat as Sind declared at 404 for five and did not have a catch or stumping either in Delhi's two totals of 130 and 89.

Sind completed a notable hat-trick by winning the final against Western India States. Batting at number 10 in Sind's total of 230, Aziz contributed 16 runs. He also effected a stumping and two catches in Western India's first innings of 66 as Sind wrapped up the match by an innings and 52 runs.

It was in between the quarter-final and semi-final of the Delhi Tournament that Aziz made his first-class debut, representing the Rest of India against the Maharajkumar of Vizianagaram's XI at the very same Roshanara ground. The three-day match, played from 13 to 15 November 1930, had been squeezed in between the two games.

The Vizianagaram XI, captained by the infamous 'Vizzy'—a future captain of India—had obtained the services of England's legendary opening pair of Jack Hobbs and Herbert Sutcliffe. Rest of India though had L. Amar Singh, one of the first great Test fast bowlers of India, opening the bowling. Aziz marked his first-class debut with a catch in the first innings and scores of four and five (not out) as Rest of India lost by 193 runs.

International Cricket

Aziz had his first taste of international cricket while representing Sind against the visiting Ceylon team at Karachi in December 1932. Opening the batting in both innings, he recorded his maiden first-class half-century (57) in the second innings of the drawn match.

A year later, he came up against the formidable English team captained by Douglas Jardine who was leading the first official Test team to tour India in 1933-34, one season after the infamous Bodyline series in Australia. Aziz was representing C.B. Rubie's XI in the two-day (non first-class) match at Karachi in October 1933.

The Ranji Trophy for the national cricket championship had been instituted in 1934-35 and in the inaugural season, Aziz played one match for Sind against Western India at Karachi in the West Zone league. Sind were defeated by four wickets in their only match and that was the end of their tournament. Bombay won the inaugural title and repeated the feat in 1935–36. Aziz again played a lone match that season against the eventual champions at Poona in which he scored his maiden Ranji Trophy fifty (65) as an opener in the second innings.

It would be a worthwhile endeavour here to take a detour into the history of the Ranji Trophy and the person after whom the tournament is named—someone with whose family both Aziz and Salim had a close association.

Ranji was none other than Colonel His Highness Shri Sir Ranjitsinhji Vibhaji, Maharajah Jam Sahib of Nawanagar—to give him his full royal title.

One of the immortals of cricket, Ranji's greatest claim to fame was that he was the inventor of the leg glance at a time in Victorian England when leg side play was considered taboo, even an anathema. Ranji thus opened up a whole new dimension of the game and the stroke now has a stamp of Indian-ness about it. Ranji was a leading member in what is generally considered cricket's Golden Age (1890 to 1914), a pantheon of immortals that includes W.G. Grace, Sydney Barnes, Wilfred Rhodes, C.B. Fry, Gilbert Jessop and Victor Trumper.

Ranji was the first Indian Test cricketer, though not the first Test cricketer born in India. He was a great favourite of English crowds at the time when India was the jewel in the crown of the vast British Empire.[12]

---

[12]Bransby Cooper, who represented Australia against England in the first Test match ever played—held at Melbourne in 1877—was born in Dacca (now Dhaka), then part of undivided India. But it was Ranji and his lustrous batting that shone a spotlight on India as he played 15 Tests for his adopted land of England between 1896 and 1902, including a spectacular 154 not out on debut against Australia at Old Trafford, Manchester.

Ranji, however, harboured a thinly veiled contempt for Indian cricket and cricketers and the release of *Batting for the Empire: A Political History of Ranjitsinhji* by Mumbai-based journalist Mario Rodrigues in 2003, a book backed by vast research and documentary evidence, showed just how intense Ranji's loyalty to the British crown was. It also exposed his disdain not just for Indian cricket but also for the independence movement led by fellow Kathiawari, Mohandas Karamchand Gandhi, who was born just three years before Ranji.[13]

Ranji's case was not unusual as the majority of the princely states back then were staunchly opposed to independence and never failed to display their fealty to the Empire. In Ranji's case, his pathway to the throne of Nawanagar was an arduous one. It was through his cricket exploits that he managed to convince the British establishment of his worthiness. A message was sent out loud and clear to the hundreds of royal houses throughout undivided India—the way to British hearts and minds was through that most traditional and beloved of sports: cricket.

Ranji, who came from very humble roots, far removed from royalty, finally achieved his life's ambition in 1907 when he ascended the throne. Behind that crowning moment though was a cesspool of intrigue and plotting. Simon Wilde in his eye-opening 1990 biography, *Ranji: A Genius Rich and Strange*, hinted darkly at an assassination plot amidst lies, deceit, thievery and extortion.

It was hoped that Ranji—who, after having retired from cricket and ascending the throne, was now spending most of his time in India—would become a patron and supporter of Indian cricket. That fond hope soon disappeared into thin air.

---

[13]See also: Ezekiel, Gulu, *Myth-Busting: Indian Cricket behind the Headlines*, Rupa Publications, New Delhi, 2021, p. 85.

The first All-India team toured England in 1911. It was funded by Tata's industrial house and organized by J.M. Framjee Patel, a former captain of the Parsi cricket team. From the start, Patel was determined to rope in Ranji as the captain, which would have been a tremendous coup on his part. But Ranji made his contempt clear. In a speech at the Parsi Ripon Club, which was reported in *The Times of India*, he poured scorn on the whole idea of such a tour.

'The imperial cricketing superstar used the occasion to tear to shreds the idea of an Indian cricket tour to Britain. "Why, Indian cricketers do not even know the ABC of the game, and an Indian team would find in England there is no county so weak that it would not score 500 runs against Indian bowling and in turn dismiss the Indian team for 30 or 40 runs," he scoffed.'[14]

Undeterred, Patel continued to plead with the Maharaja of Nawanagar to lead the side once the tour had been finalized in 1910 even though by now Ranji had long stopped playing cricket and was busy running his tiny kingdom. Ranji refused and instead recommended the 19-year-old Maharaja of Patiala, Bhupinder Singh, whose father Rajinder had been a staunch supporter of Ranji during his most difficult times when he was heavily in debt.[15]

---

[14]*The Times of India*, 25 January 1904.
[15]Contrary to the popular myth, Patiala was not involved in any aspect of the tour. This particular myth has been busted in Prashant Kidambi's book *Cricket Country: The Untold History of the First all India Team*, Penguin Viking. In fact his main reason for going on the tour with his vast entourage was to attend the coronation of King George V in London. As a result he played just two matches.

Ranji's Refusal

When India made their bow in international cricket, the fledgling BCCI was keen on Ranji's equally brilliant nephew K.S. Duleepsinhji leading the side in the 1932 Lord's Test. Duleep had already played 12 Tests for England between 1929 and 1931 with the fantastic average of 58.52. But poor health had cut short his career and besides, Ranji forbade Duleep from playing for India saying, 'Duleep and I are English cricketers.'

No wonder A.S. de Mello, the first secretary of the BCCI, wrote in exasperation, 'Yet, and I tell it with deep regret, Ranjitsinhji was never at any stage prepared to combine his roles of sportsman and Indian prince [...] Ranji, in fact, did absolutely nothing for Indian sport and sportsmen.'[16]

De Mello's frustrations were perhaps understandable. But it must be acknowledged that Ranji did play a big part in discovering and nurturing the talents of L. Amar Singh and recommended him for that first tour of England. Amar Singh formed a formidable opening partnership with Mohammad Nissar in the 1930s, making India one of the leading fast bowling nations in the era before Independence and Partition. Ranji and his successors looked after both Amar and his elder brother and fellow fast bowler L. Ramji, who came from impoverished backgrounds. They were provided employment, housing and support, which made them intensely loyal to the House of Nawanagar. Duleep, on the other hand, contributed much to India and Indian cricket in numerous ways. Almost all the leading Indian cricketers at the time were in the employ of one princely state or the other when funds were sparse.

But how genuine was the patronage of the royals which was at its peak as Indian cricket was beginning to find its feet in

---

[16]de Mello, Anthony, *Portrait of Indian Sport*, Macmillan, New Delhi, 1959, p. 16.

the 1920s and 30s? There were obvious strings attached. As we have seen with Ranji's example, supporting cricket was a quick route to curry favour with the Crown. There was also ego and prestige, with the princes bringing over legendary names from England and Australia to strengthen their squads as one royal XI took on another in fierce battle—surely the precursor to that festival of money and cricket: the mega-rich IPL.

These royal egos, while providing employment to cricketers, also engaged in unseemly squabbles and politics which earned Indian cricket a bad name, none more so than Vizzy, who inveigled his way to the captaincy of the national team for the 1936 tour of England, one of the most disastrous in cricket history.

The maiden tour of India by England in 1933–34 saw Bhupinder Singh Patiala and Vizzy jockey for power and position following the passing of Ranji in 1933. By now, the BCCI felt the need for a national championship to augment the Bombay Pentangular tournament. In the board meeting in Simla in 1934, Bhupinder made his generous offer—he would sponsor the tournament, but it should be named after Ranji, his old family friend.[17]

But Vizzy would not be thwarted. He proposed the trophy should be named after Lord Willingdon, the then Viceroy of India and a patron of the BCCI, and not Ranji who, echoing the words of de Mello, Vizzy said had done nothing for Indian cricket. Vizzy's proposal was accepted and the grand trophy which he donated was put on display. Patiala could only look on helplessly.

Now a campaign began in the Indian media supporting the idea of naming the trophy after Ranji rather than Willingdon. Mahatma Gandhi had begun the Civil Disobedience movement

---

[17]Majumdar, Boria, 'Palace Intrigue', *Wisden Asia Cricket,* September 2002.

against the British in 1930 and nationalist feelings were running high.

It was finally Patiala who had the last laugh in this particular tussle. Bombay, winners of the inaugural title for 1934–35, were presented with the Ranji Trophy in New Delhi by Lord Willingdon himself. Vizzy's Willingdon Trophy was consigned to a minor tournament.

Patiala had pulled the rabbit out of the hat by his offer to sponsor the visit of Jack Ryder's Australian side to India in 1935–36, which was to be a selection trial for the Indian team to England in 1936—and thereby hangs a tale. Not only did Abdul Aziz have the honour of being a member of the Nawanagar team that won the Ranji Trophy in 1936–37, he also donned national colours for the first and only time against Ryder's Australians the previous season.

And it was Ranji's successor to the throne, Jam Sahib Digvijaysinhji, who brought Aziz from Karachi to Nawanagar in 1935 to strengthen his cricket team.

As for the Vizzy/Patiala internecine clash, while Patiala won the battle for the naming of the national trophy, his bitter rival won the war when he was named captain for the 1936 series in England. And his manager was none other than Jack Brittain-Jones. But that is another story for another day.

The First Aussies

In bringing the first Australian cricketers to play in India, Patiala was greatly assisted by the Melbourne-born brilliant all-rounder Frank Tarrant, one of the greatest cricketers to never play a Test match. For cricketing matters, he was Bhupinder's right-hand man and it was his tireless efforts against a recalcitrant Australian Board of Control for International Cricket (now Cricket Australia) that finally succeeded in bringing a motley bunch of cricketers—some retired in their forties, some young and still to make a name for themselves—to India for a tour lasting nearly five months, from October 1935 to February 1936. The official Australian Test team was touring South Africa at the same time and the main concern of the authorities was that the team to India should not be mistaken to be the official Australian team side since it was a private tour. It was therefore named 'The Maharaja of Patiala's Team of Australian Cricketers'.

This was the start of the India/Australia cricket journey that today is bidding to replace the traditional 'Ashes' series between England and Australia as the pre-eminent world cricket fixture. No wonder Megan Ponsford titled her fascinating account of the tour in her 2022 book *The Has-Beens and Never-Will-Bes: A Boy's Own Adventure of Australian Cricket and the Raj*.[18]

Patiala's immense wealth bankrolled the tour and his contribution of £10,000—a vast amount back then—took care of all expenses including players' fees.

The visiting side was led by Jack Ryder, aged 46, a former captain of Australia who played his last Test six years before the India tour. His deputy was the 49-year-old Charlie Macartney, who was dubbed the 'Governor General' for his stylish batting. Despite the presence of a few youngsters in the touring party, the average age was 40. Their aim was ostensibly to prepare the Indians for their forthcoming tour of England and act as selection trials for the 1936 series where they would play three Tests abroad for the first time. The first tour in 1932 had consisted of a one-off Test at Lord's.

Among Indian cricketers, administrators and fans, the visitors were considered pushovers. But that was not to be.

---

[18]The author is the granddaughter of Bill Ponsford, one of the all-time batting greats. Her grand-uncle, Tom Leather, was on the tour and the book is based on his collection of photos and cuttings of the historic trip.

They gave a grand account of themselves, drawing the series of four unofficial Test matches 2-2. They won 11 of their 23 matches, of which 17 had first-class status, drew nine and lost three, including two of the unofficial Tests against strong Indian combinations.

Aziz first encountered the Aussies while representing Sind at Karachi before the first Test. It was a rout lasting two days—the tourists won by an innings and 90 runs. Aziz, opening the batting in both innings, top scored in the first (26) as Sind were dismissed for 79, made tediously in 56.4 overs over a span of more than three hours. Fast bowlers Lisle Nagel and Ron Oxenham did all the damage with five wickets apiece.

The Australians replied with 294 and Sind did only marginally better the second time around—they were all out for 125. Oxenham, who would be the leading bowler on tour, claimed five wickets again.

Macartney was contracted to write on the tour for the venerable Madras daily *The Hindu*. In his report on the first day's play, he was critical of the defensive approach of the Sind batsmen, including Aziz.

'The Sind Eleven gave a very restrained exhibition of batting today and failed badly, opposed to the accurate bowling of the Australians [...] Certainly Oxenham and Nagel operated steadily and skillfully, but if batsmen are going to allow bowlers to hold them up indefinitely, then big totals or entertaining batting will not be their reward. Abdul Aziz employed all the cautious methods possible for a batsman but on this occasion defensive measures were entirely wrong.'[19]

He did, however, have a word of praise for Aziz's work behind the stumps. Australia lost three wickets by close of the

---

[19]Macartney, C.G., 'Need for More Enterprise; Sind Batsmen's Defects; Australians Well Placed; Nagel and Oxenham Play Havoc', *The Hindu*, 23 November 1935.

first day and one of those was of captain Ryder, stumped by Aziz off the bowling of off spinner Mobed.

'Ryder was stumped magnificently by Abdul Aziz and his rapidity in execution on this occasion was surprising.'[20]

There was more praise for his performance on the second day. 'Some of the returns to the wicket were reckless, and at times unnecessarily speedy. In this respect, the wicket-keeping of Aziz was excellent for not only did he retain his good style and effectiveness throughout Australia's innings but he gathered these awkward returns to the wicket remarkably well. He also cleverly and smartly stumped [Hampden 'Hammy'] Love when that batsman was well set and causing trouble.'[21]

Aziz pulled off a total of three stumpings including that of Fred Mair, but in Sind's second innings he could only contribute six runs with the bat.

Navle, who had kept wickets in the 1932 Lord's Test, opened the batting in the first 'Test' at Bombay but was replaced behind the stumps by Aziz for the second at Calcutta. Aziz was in turn replaced by Khershed Meherhomji for the third 'Test', and then S.V.T. Chari came in for the fourth as the selectors looked to decide which wicketkeepers to send to England in 1936. In the end, they went with Dattaram Hindlekar, Meherhomji and Dilawar Hussain, each of whom played one Test in the series.

Aziz, in his lone 'Test' at Calcutta, was zero not out in the first innings batting at number nine as the Indians were routed for a paltry 48 all out, and was then promoted to open in the second, scoring 12 as the tourists romped home by eight wickets. Aziz claimed one catch in both innings. Six Indian batsmen failed to score in the first innings with Macartney (as well as Oxenham) claiming five wickets with his rarely used

---
[20]Ibid.
[21]Ibid.

left-arm spin, the Indians being put in on a damp pitch after heavy overnight rain.

Macartney in his report in *The Hindu* lauded Captain Nayudu's decision to move Aziz up to open the innings, noting his defensive technique was an asset at the top of the order, 'His 12 runs were much more valuable than they appear on paper.'[22]

Thus ended Abdul Aziz's brief international career.[23]

Like father, like son? Not quite. Though Salim did briefly keep wickets for Rajasthan in the late 1950s before discarding the big gloves, by all accounts, Aziz was a defensive batsman, something his son most certainly was not.

So how good was Aziz as a wicketkeeper? At over 6 ft (Salim was 6 ft 1 in.) and around 220 pounds, he was big and burly (unlike Salim, who kept a slim figure right till the end), unusual for a 'keeper. But he stood up to the stumps to Amar Singh, Mubarak Ali and Shute Banerjee, all considerably quick, and was also impressive against the left-arm spin of Mankad.

Aziz's Ranji Exploits

When Nawanagar made their debut in the Ranji Trophy in the championship's third season in 1936–37, the Jam Sahib spared no effort or expense in rounding up a formidable team—after all, the trophy was named after his uncle and his predecessor as ruler.

Apart from Aziz, he also recruited batsman Nariman Marshall (who had toured England in 1932 without ever playing a Test), as well as Test player Sorabji Colah and India's pace ace Amar

---

[22]Macartney, C.G., 'Fighting Innings by Amarnath; Fortune Frowns on India', *The Hindu*, 2 January 1936.

[23]He did play a match against Lord Tennyson's English team on their 1937–38 tour of India but that was a tour match for Jam Sahib of Jam Nagar's XI at Jamnagar and not an unofficial Test.

Singh, both of whom played for Western India the previous season. This was the first Ranji Trophy season for Mankad, who was still a decade away from making his Test debut.

Nawanagar's first match in the West Zone was against Sind, Aziz's former team. Aziz did not do much as Nawanagar impressively won their maiden Ranji Trophy match by 252 runs.

Bombay, the reigning champions who had won the title in the first two years of the championship, were formidable opponents in Nawanagar's next match at Poona, and this is where Aziz excelled. The match was drawn with Nawanagar gaining the first innings lead. The team was led by Sussex professional Albert Wensley, who had been brought over by the Jam Sahib to coach the team. He replaced as captain the Jam's relative R.K. Yadvendrasinhji who had led in the opening match. The young prince was taking no chances and nepotism was not going to sway him.

Talking of nepotism, Amar's brother Ramji was one of the umpires at Poona, which must have led to some awkward moments at the very least.

Opening with Mankad, Aziz recorded the highest score of his first-class career, his 89 ground out in 270 minutes being Nawanagar's top score in the match which they came close to losing. Amar Singh's fiery bowling (eight for 62) saw Bombay all out for 174, to which Nawanagar replied with 263.

With Vijay Merchant propping up Bombay's second innings 277, Nawanagar were set a target of 189 and after Aziz was first out for a duck, they collapsed to 73 for seven before Amar and Yadavendrasinhji held out for a draw with an unbeaten stand worth 67 runs. The zonal final at Poona once again saw Nawanagar claim first innings honours against Western India in a drawn game. They received a walk-over from United Provinces in the semi-final and were now in the final against Bengal in Bombay.

The Jam's Trickery

How determined was the Jam to win the title? Enough to snatch away Bengal's star medium pacer Shute Banerjee on the eve of the final.

Former Bengal and East Zone captain and author Raju Mukherji recounted the act of sabotage, 'On the eve of the match Nawanagar offered Banerjee a job with the condition that he had to join service from the very next morning itself, which happened to be the first day of the final! The offer was couched in such a manner that Banerjee would not be able to play against Nawanagar.'[24]

The offer put the young man—who had toured England in both 1936 and 1946 and played just one Test match in a storied career—in a pickle as he was unemployed at the time and job security was essential. Bengal captain and wicketkeeper Paul van der Gucht appealed to Wensley—both were English county cricketers—but to no avail, as the orders had come from no less than the Jam Sahib. Banerjee had to miss the final altogether as he was not qualified at that stage to represent Nawanagar either.

Nawanagar won by 256 runs. And thus Aziz achieved what his more illustrious son could never do—be a part of a Ranji Trophy-winning team. Salim, on six occasions, was a member of the star-studded Rajasthan in a Ranji final, but each time he ended up being on the losing side. He played 29 official Tests, his father none. But the Ranji Trophy defeats rankled Salim throughout his life.

With pace bowlers Amar Singh, Banerjee and Mubarak Ali, as well as left-arm spinner Mankad in their ranks, Nawanagar now had the most potent bowling attack in the country and they once again reached the Ranji Trophy final in the 1937–38

---

[24]Mukherji, Raju, *Cricket India: Tales Untold: Controversies and Contributions*, Notion Press, Chennai, 2020.

season at Bombay. But this time they lost to Hyderabad by a solitary wicket in a thrilling encounter.

Aziz's final first-class match came in the 1938–39 season against Sind at Karachi, as Nawanagar this time failed to make the semi-finals. Thus ended his brief career of 19 first-class matches stretching from 1930 to 1938. He finished with 394 runs at 14.59 from 31 innings (three half- centuries, highest score 89) and claimed 23 catches and 11 stumpings.

Aziz was still in the employ of the Nawanagar royal family. He was with the police in the kingdom and was also employed as a coach. But then came Independence and Partition and all the turmoil and tragedy that it left in its chaotic wake.

Nawanagar was among the first princely states to sign the Instrument of Accession after Independence. In 1949, Nawanagar and the adjoining princely states merged into the new state of Saurashtra. In 1959, Nawanagar became known as Jamnagar and a year later it became part of the new state of Gujarat on the division of the Bombay State.

The Separation

With all these historic changes happening around him, Digvijaysinhji had a lot on his plate. The Nawanagar team was in fact disbanded, the 1947–48 season being their last. The Jam Sahib even represented India at the United Nations. Cricket was no longer one of his pet projects and quite understandably so.

Aziz would not have been the only ex-cricketer struggling for survival at this time. His birthday, 15 August, was certainly an auspicious one, but at the birth of independent India and the new nation of Pakistan, he was torn as to what his future would hold—at 42 years of age, his playing days were behind him.

Many Muslim families were split at the time of Partition. The Pataudi royal family saw Iftikhar Ali Khan stay in India while one sister's family moved to Pakistan. Some Muslim cricketers who had represented India in Test matches pre-1947 went on to play for Pakistan. A future Pakistan captain, Asif Iqbal, left India as late as the 1960s.

Aziz moved to Karachi, where he had good contacts, having learned his cricket there and represented Sind in the Ranji Trophy before his move to the now-renamed Nawanagar. His hope perhaps was to get some gainful employment. But why did he leave his wife (who went on to become head nurse at a Jamnagar hospital), two sons—Salim and the younger Jehangir—and three daughters behind? The exact circumstances are unknown even now since it was a touchy subject and was rarely broached either with Abdul or Salim during their lifetimes.

Pakistan's premier batsman, Hanif Mohammed, wrote in his autobiography how he was discovered as a schoolboy in Karachi by the coach who became known in Pakistan as 'Master Aziz'. 'He had migrated to Pakistan in 1947, leaving his family behind in India. He was separated from his wife, a fact which caused him a lot of distress.'[25]

Hanif went on to write that Aziz spent all his money on his students, which included Hanif's brothers Raees, Wazir, Mushtaq and Sadiq, three of whom also played Test cricket. The now-penniless Aziz would ask for money for food. 'For us he was like a father figure and an angel. I am yet to meet anyone like him.'[26] There is also a photo of the massive Master Aziz towering over the original Little Master of subcontinental cricket. Hanif's words also open the possibility that he left the family behind due to a marital falling-out.

---

[25]Mohammed, Hanif, *Playing for Pakistan: An Autobiography*, self-published, Karachi, 1999.
[26]Ibid.

Aziz was a coach at the Sind Madrassah-tul-Islam where he also lived in a small room and where Mohammed Ali Jinnah had been a student. For three decades, he was a mentor to many other famous Pakistani cricketers and was also attached to the Board of Control for Cricket in Pakistan (BCCP) as a coach.

There is a chapter on Master Aziz titled 'The Many Sons of Master Aziz' in a book on Pakistan cricket by Richard Heller and Peter Oborne.[27] The writers speculate that the separation of the father from his family may have had 'a deep psychological influence' on Aziz and undoubtedly on Salim as well. The abandonment must have been the reason why Salim took up his maternal surname of Durani out of loyalty to his mother. There is reason to believe that Salim's personal choices with regards to his own family, his restlessness in employment and shifting from city to city, may also have stemmed from this childhood trauma, as well as his shaky relationship with personal finances.

Their only meeting after Aziz's departure for Pakistan was at Calcutta during the fourth Test on England's 1961–62 tour, where Salim did the star turn with eight wickets in the match as India won by 187 runs.

Heller and Oborne, quoting Pakistani cricket personalities, paint a sad picture of a man who was eccentric, absent-minded and perennially struggling for money—he was 'disorganized and disconnected' as they put it.[28] He was invited to the Karachi Test of 1978 by the touring Indian team and met the players. But a year later, he was dead, penniless and forgotten. It was a tragic end to—despite his cricket exploits—a sad life.

---

[27]Heller, Richard, and Peter Oborne, *White on Green: Celebrating the Drama of Pakistan Cricket*, Simon & Schuster UK, Great Britain, 2016, p. 30.
[28]Ibid.

Two

Climbing the Ladder (1950–51 to 1959–60)

Every journey begins with a single step, as the saying goes. Baby Salim's began with his doting father passing a cricket ball back and forth across his eyes to get him used to the sight of the red cherry. And thus the infant's destiny was sealed. Cricket was to be his life. It was only a matter of time, effort and generous dollops of destiny.

Like countless kids before and after him though, Salim's first playing experience was with a tennis ball. His father was his first coach and when father bowled to son, Salim's mother played the role of wicketkeeper—a family trait for sure.

It was Abdul who converted Salim from a right-hander to a left-hander, thus exploding the myth that the adult Salim Durani was a natural left-hander as he was often described during his illustrious career.

'I am a freak left-hander,' Durani told Harish Munwani. 'The Gods had decreed that I be a right-hander and had it not been for an incident that occurred when I was eight-years-old, I would have remained a right-hander for life. And for that matter, maybe a farmer. Not an international cricketer [...]'[29]

Abdul was keen that his son switch from being naturally

---

[29]Munwani, Harish, 'My Cricketing Years', *Sportsworld*, 1 November 1978.

right-handed to becoming a left-hander. The reasoning, according to Salim, was sound—Abdul felt that left-handers had a distinct advantage, since there were so few of them around.[30]

The experiment was first tried on his younger brother, Jehangir. But he lacked an interest in cricket, and so Abdul turned his attention to young Salim. It was to Vinoo Mankad that Abdul turned for advice—someone who would play a guiding role in Salim's life and career for four decades.

'Vinoo bhai suggested that my right hand be tied behind my back, thereby forcing me to do everything with my left hand—the unnatural hand. The gimmick worked and soon I forgot to do anything with my right hand,' Durani told Munwani.[31]

It was Mankad who took the youngster under his wing from the age of nine or 10. 'After that [Abdul's early coaching] I came under the guidance of the great Vinoo Mankad. This was the most important stage of my development as I learnt a great deal from him. I patterned my bowling also on him and he was the man who taught me everything about orthodox left-arm bowling.'[32]

After excelling in the all-Saurashtra inter-school tournament, Salim was picked for the state schools side in the All-India Cooch Behar Schools Tournament in 1950–51.

The trophy was donated by the Maharaja of Cooch Behar. From 1945–46 to 1986–87 it was played by schools, but after that it was changed to an under-19 tournament and was competed in by the majority of the Ranji Trophy teams. Many budding

---

[30]Two decades later, Lala Amarnath, the first captain of independent India, made the same switch with his eldest son Surinder and for the same reason. As a flamboyant left-handed batsman like Durani, Surinder played 10 Test matches between 1976 and 1978. Lala and Surinder are still the only father-son pair to both score centuries on their Test debuts.
[31]Munwani, Harish, 'My Cricketing Years', *Sportsworld*, 1 November 1978.
[32]Memon, Ayaz, 'Mr Sixer', *Cricketer Asia*, July 1983.

cricketers first made their name on the national stage in this tournament before going on to bigger things. It was considered the stepping stone to first-class cricket but has faded out with the rise of the Indian Premier League since 2008.

According to Raju Mukherji, the Maharajah of Cooch Behar, Nripendra Narayan Bhup Bahadur (1862–1911), was the foremost patron of cricket in Bengal in the 1890s. It was his grandson Jagaddipendra Narayan (1915–70), the last ruler who led Bengal in the Ranji Trophy in the 1940s, who had donated the trophy.[33, 34]

Salim got his name in print in a national daily for the first time in that 1950–51 championship. In January 1951, Saurashtra Combined Schools lost their lone match to Bombay Combined Schools by seven wickets at Rajkot. But it was the 16-year-old Salim who caught the eye of the Bombay coach with a sterling all-round display.

Saurashtra scored 194 and 107 with Bombay—led by future Test captain Nari Contractor—replying with 265 and 45 for three. Salim scored 41 and took five wickets for 98 runs in the first innings. During a dinner for the teams hosted by the Thakore Saheb of Rajkot, Salim was approached by Yusuf Farid, the manager of the Bombay team and also the teacher-cum-coach of the famed Anjuman-E-Islam High School, one of Bombay's leading cricket schools. He invited him to Bombay to join the school and take part in the Lord Harris Shield tournament for schools. Salim sought his mother's permission to move from Jamnagar to Bombay. She was persuaded to do

---

[33]Mukherji, Raju, *Cricket India: Tales Untold: Controversies and Contributions*, Notion Press, Chennai, 2020.

[34]I am indebted to author and historian Trinanjan Chakraborty for helping me get access to the reports of the Cooch Behar Trophy from the National Library in Alipore, Kolkata. The scores are neither available online nor in *Indian Cricket*.

so by Mankad, who cared for Salim like his own son during his initial stay in the city.³⁵

Salim never completed his schooling but made his mark in the various Bombay tournaments before returning to Jamnagar.

The next season (1951–52), having shifted to Bombay, Salim represented Bombay Combined Schools in the championship. And this time his team reached the final at Eden Gardens in February 1952—his first visit to the fabled ground where he would attain a cult hero status over the years. A photo of the team shows Salim towering over his teammates, something he would do for the rest of his career.

In the semi-finals, Bombay trounced Bengal by an innings and 112 runs, while National Defence Academy (NDA) beat Hyderabad to reach the final. Once again, Salim found himself on the losing side and once again he was the star performer.

'Bombay's Salim Deadly on the Opening Day' was the headline in *The Times of India* for the *PTI* report on the opening day, 28 February. National Defence Academy scored 339 and Bombay replied with 13 for the loss of one wicket. Captain Sukdhip Grewal scored 184 while Durani captured six wickets for 106 runs with his left arm spin.

Bombay replied the next day with 200 all out to concede a big first innings lead. National Defence Academy, by stumps on the second day, reached 51 for five with Salim picking up four of those five. He would finish with four for 33 as Grewal (177) completed the feat of a century in both innings, NDA all out for 274, setting Bombay the formidable target of 413. On the fourth day, they were all out for 260, losing by 153 runs. One of Salim's teammates, incidentally, was Sopan Sardesai, cousin

---

³⁵As narrated by Saurashtra Ranji Trophy player Vaman Jani: 'An Enigma Wrapped in Controversy', http://tinyurl.com/53cwradt. Accessed on 30 May 2023.

of Test batsman Dilip, with whom Salim forged a strong bond over two tours to the Caribbean in 1962 and 1971.

The report on the final day stated that the trophy was still in Sind, who had won it before Partition. 'A representative of the Pakistan Cricket Association, however, has promised that the trophy is duly returned.'[36]

Salim's move to Bombay paid dividends both for himself and his school. Anjuman won the Lord Harris Shield title nine seasons on the trot between 1946–47 and 1954–55.

In the 1952–53 final against Bai Kabibai High School, he had figures of five for 49 as his school won the title for the seventh straight year. The same season in the second round, he recorded his highest score of 183 against Ideal High School. The very next season he would make his first-class debut in the Ranji Trophy, and a memorable one at that.

Some of Bombay's—and India's—greatest cricketers cut their teeth in the Harris Shield—Vijay Merchant, Sunil Gavaskar, Dilip Vengsarkar, Ravi Shastri, Wasim Jaffer, Sanjay Manjrekar and Sachin Tendulkar, to name just a few. The highest individual score in the tournament is 546 in 2013 by Test cricketer Prithvi Shaw.

The tournament, which celebrated its centenary in 1997—making it the oldest continuously run tournament in India—shot into the world cricket headlines when two fresh-faced schoolboys entered the record books with the highest partnership in cricket history.

Tendulkar and Vinod Kambli added 664 runs unbroken for the third wicket for Sharadashram Vidyamandir (English) against St Xavier's (Fort) in the semi-finals in 1987–88, both scoring unbeaten triple centuries. Tendulkar captained his school in the final—in which he scored another unbeaten triple hundred—against Anjuman, which saw the two teams emerge joint winners

---

[36] 'National Defence Academy Win Championship', *The Statesman*, 3 March 1952.

as the first innings could not be completed. In the next season, he led them to victory in the final against the same school.

Brilliant Debut

The leap from school cricket to first-class cricket for Salim (this is how his name appeared in scorecards in the early 1950s before he took on the Durani surname) came about for Saurashtra against Gujarat at the Commerce College Ground, Navrangupura, Ahmedabad (now known as HL Commerce College), on 28–30 November 1953. He was two weeks shy of his nineteenth birthday and made an immediate and dramatic impact.

Gujarat were a strong team with five current or future Test cricketers among their ranks. It was Saurashtra's only match of the season in which they conceded the first innings lead to Gujarat, led by Jasu Patel, who would make his Test debut three years later. His counterpart was R.K. Indravijaysinhji of the Ranji royal family.

On the first day, Gujarat were dismissed for 225 (Salim zero for 18 off four overs) and by stumps Saurashtra had reached 103 for two, Salim batting on 56.

He completed his century (108) on the second day with Saurashtra falling short by 18 runs on first innings. He batted for 150 minutes with 17 boundaries and was the only batsman who stood up to Patel's off spin (six for 57 from 26 overs), the next highest score being 25 by Kutubuddin.

The report in *Indian Cricket* for 1953–54 noted, 'A feature of Saurashtra's batting was the fine play by Salim, an 18-year-old schoolboy from Jamnagar [...] he was the only player to withstand the accurate off spin bowling of Jasu Patel.'[37]

---

[37]*Indian Cricket for 1953–54*, Gurunathan, S.K. (ed.), Kasturi & Sons Ltd, Madras, 1954, p. 124.

Salim was the top scorer in the second innings too with 41. It was thus a memorable Ranji Trophy/first-class debut for the teenager.

That was also the only match Salim would play for Saurashtra. The very next season he switched allegiances to Gujarat, lured away by their captain Patel, so impressed was he by the youngster's performance. He would go on to play a pivotal though unwitting part in Salim's career in January 1960.

Salim's lone match for Gujarat in the 1954–55 season was against Baroda in December 1954. Once again, he impressed with his score of 72. Gujarat scored 354 but bowed out to Baroda who replied with 413 for four, Salim again going wicket-less as Gujarat tried out 10 bowlers.

He got his first taste of international cricket the next season (1955–56) against New Zealand in their maiden series against India. Playing for an 'Indian XI'—virtually a Test team—Durani bagged the first pair of his first-class career. Both times he fell to medium pacer Harry Cave, the Kiwi captain. The match was played on coir matting at Ahmedabad. 'I was very disappointed,' he told G. Viswanath. 'Cave was moving the ball out. I could not cope with the two deliveries.'[38]

There were just two matches for Gujarat in the Ranji Trophy that season. In his fourth first-class match, he got his maiden wicket. Ironically, it was a member of the Ranji royal family that had given both him and his father their first big breaks in cricket in Nawanagar. Manoharsinhji Pradyumansinhji, the Thakore Saheb of Rajkot, was caught by Vinayak Desai in the first innings in the only over Salim bowled. Gujarat took first innings points in this match.

Their next match in the West Zone league was against

---

[38] Viswanath, G, 'I Would Have Succeeded in ODIs, T20s', *Sportstar*, 9 January 2021.

Bombay. It would be the first of many encounters Salim would have against the formidable Ranji Trophy champions, in none of which he emerged on the winning side. However, he impressed once again, for Gujarat in the match with 74 not out in the first innings. Bombay took the first innings points and Gujarat conceded the match midway through the third and final day.

Now would begin the fabled journey for Salim Durani in the Rajasthan team, a glorious one full of triumphs and heartbreaks that lasted 21 seasons from 1956–57 to 1977–78. For after just a single match for Saurashtra and two seasons with Gujarat, Salim had once again jumped ship.

In a lovely twist, his teammate in Rajasthan was none other than the mighty Vinoo Mankad, Salim's guru and mentor who had been his father's teammate exactly 20 seasons earlier in 1936–37, when Nawanagar won the Ranji Trophy for the first and only time. Another familiar face was wicketkeeper Sopan Sardesai, his teammate from the Cooch Behar days.

Rajputana—which included parts of modern-day Gujarat and Madhya Pradesh—was part of the Ranji Trophy from 1935–36 till 1955–56 save for two seasons—1941–42 and then 1951–52—when they were replaced by the newly formed state of Rajasthan into which it was merged in March 1949. By 1956–57, Rajasthan in turn replaced the former princely state and they have been a fixture in the Ranji Trophy ever since.

The one constant in all this chopping and changing was His Highness Bhagwat Singh of Mewar, the Maharana of Udaipur. He made his first-class debut for Rajputana in 1945–46 and at the age of just 18 was captain of the side, something which royalty back then expected as a divine right. He was a mere prince at the time, ascending the throne in 1955.

The Rajasthan line-up when they made their comeback in the tournament after five seasons would have been unrecognizable to a local cricket fan, packed as it was with big names poached from other teams. The BCCI had given permission to each team to field two professionals, and in the side were Mankad and G.S. Ramchand, both Test cricketers who had played for Bombay in the previous season.

Other unfamiliar faces, apart from Durani, were Bhausaheb Nimbalkar and Sayajirao Dhanawade, an accomplished all-rounder. Both of them had represented Madhya Bharat the previous season, though it was for Maharashtra that Nimbalkar recorded his mammoth 443 not out, which remains the highest first-class score by an Indian even 75 years later.

The Rajasthan Saga

For Durani, this was his third team in a matter of four years in the Ranji Trophy, early evidence of his gypsy-like nature which would be the one constant in his life even after his playing days were long past. But then, being a non-matriculate, his only source of income was cricket and the Rajasthan offer was undoubtedly too good to refuse.

Now all these players were representing Rajasthan against Madhya Bharat in their opening match of the new 1956–57 season at the Yeshwant ground in Indore, a needle encounter for sure. Sure enough, trouble flared up on the eve of the match when Madhya Bharat objected to the presence of some of the outstation players in the Rajasthan squad.

N.S. Ramaswami in his summary of the 1956–57 season in the *Indian Cricket* condemned this constant movement of players from one team to another as 'evil'.[39] He called for stricter measures to be enforced by the BCCI, saying the players were allowed to change states with bewildering rapidity which led to

---

[39]Ramaswami, N.S., 'Notes on the Season 1956–57, Bombay Retain Championships', *Indian Cricket 1956–57*, Guranathan, S.K. (ed.), Kasturi & Sons Private Ltd, Madras, 1958, p. 82.

unseemliness and confusion. While not specifically mentioning Rajasthan, it appeared theirs was the most glaring example of this trend though other teams were also guilty of the same.

Ramaswami's concerns were genuine. In the 1946–47 season, there was the unprecedented situation of a match having to be replayed. The reason: Kathiawar, who defeated Gujarat by six runs at Rajkot in December 1946, had in their team G. Kishenchand who was not qualified to play for them. He had played for Sind in the previous season and permission was gained from the BCCI for his inclusion only after the toss had been made. This was against the laws and Gujarat played the match under protest.

The BCCI cancelled the result of the match and a replay was ordered at the same venue in January 1947. The tables were now turned and Gujarat won the replayed match by an innings and 32 runs. The original match was cancelled from the Ranji Trophy records and reclassified as a 'first-class friendly' match—a contradiction in terms if ever there was one.

Durani's own move was engineered by Maharana Bhagwat Singh, who continued to captain Rajasthan more than 10 years after his debut. He was determined to see Rajasthan win the Ranji Trophy during his lifetime and spared no expense to rope in the big names of Indian cricket including, later, Vijay Manjrekar, Subhash Gupte and Rusi Surti.

Sadly for the erstwhile ruler, who vowed to go to Haridwar and take a dip in the holy Ganges if and when Rajasthan won the title, this never happened in his lifetime. He died in 1984, after seeing Rajasthan come agonizingly close to victory season after season.

The chief cricket advisor to the Maharana was Raj Singh Dungarpur. He was also royalty as it was back then and a prime mover behind the success of Rajasthan cricket, for whom he played as a pace bowler and captain. Raj Singh also played a major part in Durani's life post cricket and later assumed numerous senior roles in the BCCI.

Kishan Rungta, a future captain of Rajasthan, who died in 2021, was also playing his first match for Rajasthan having played one match for Maharashtra the previous season. The family business was based in Rajasthan, so his transition was smooth. His family would dominate Rajasthan and Indian cricket administration for decades.

He described the playing conditions in Udaipur as 'feudal', with practice facilities in the palace compound overshadowed by the magnificent Udaipur Palace on the left and Lake Pichola on the right.[40] Rungta gave a lot of credit to Raj Singh for advancing cricket in Rajasthan once the Maharana had taken over as president of the Rajasthan Cricket Association (RCA).

The reorganized and revitalized RCA's first match of the season was a grudge match for Raj Singh, who felt he had not been treated well by Madhya Bharat for whom, like Rungta, he had made his debut the previous season. According to Rungta, Raj Singh spent a sleepless night before the match as he was determined that Rajasthan teach Madhya Bharat a fitting lesson for his alleged humiliation. He persuaded Bhagwat Singh to offer the players—nearly all of them professionals—an added incentive, that of a rupee for every run they scored.

The match turned out to be a no-contest. The star-studded Rajasthan won by an innings and 319 runs. Madhya Bharat succumbed to 91 and 184 in reply to Rajasthan's mammoth 594 for eight declared with centuries by Arjun Singh and Rungta (who did not accept the monetary reward as he was one of the amateurs in the side) and 88 by Durani, who also scalped three wickets in Madhya Bharat's second innings.

---

[40]Rungta, Kishan Gupta, *Raj Singh Dungarpur: A Tribute*, Samar Singh and Harsh Vardhan (eds.), Popular Prakashan, Mumbai, 2014, p. 113.

There was another fallout of the match. The teenaged Hanumant Singh had impressed for Madhya Bharat on his debut with scores of 14 not out and 61, and so had the medium pacer Arjun Naidu (three for 82). You guessed it—they were both 'kidnapped' by Rajasthan![41]

Hanumant, nephew of Duleep and grand-nephew of Ranji, was royalty from Rajasthan and hence fitted in well with the team milieu. In 1964, he became the third cricketer of royal lineage to score a century on Test debut (in his case against England), following that of his great-uncle Ranji as well as Iftikhar Ali Khan Pataudi, both for England against Australia. By a strange coincidence, two other royals, Iftikhar's son, Mansoor, and Duleep also scored centuries in their first Tests against Australia, though these were not on Test debuts.

Veteran sports administrator Amrit Mathur grew up following Rajasthan's Ranji Trophy fortunes during their golden years. He wrote about the team of the 1960s, 'This was the famous "Singhji" Rajasthan Ranji side which was dominated by members of the royalty. The joke was that the royals selected themselves and commoners filled the remaining slots.'

Mathur also had an amusing take on the bowling of Raj Singh, '[He] ran in from close to the sightscreen to bowl gentle outswing.'[42]

Durani 'Arrives'

Durani had well and truly arrived on the national stage and so, it appears, had Rajasthan. But the newfangled team riding on a high after their innings victory was brought crashing down to earth in its very next match. Up against Uttar Pradesh at

---

[41]Ibid.
[42]Mathur, Amrit, *Pitchside: My Life in Indian Cricket*, Westland Books, Chennai, 2023, p. 9.

Benares, they were met by a rampaging C.K. Nayudu, who at 61 years carted the Rajasthan bowlers all across the ground in smashing 84 runs including two sixes, his son C.N. 'Bobjee' Nayudu chipping in with 72. To add to the family fun, C.K.'s brother, C.S. Nayudu, was the standout bowler with six wickets as Rajasthan conceded a lead of 54 runs.

In the lead-up to the match, Mankad coached his bowlers to hurl bouncers at C.K., against whom he held a grudge—we shall soon discover why. But C.K. met fire with fire.

When Uttar Pradesh reached 342 for five on the third day—10 Rajasthan players having bowled—Bhagwat Singh conceded the match with a full day remaining. It was a poor gesture, one that was condemned all round. There had been an epidemic of such acts in the championship over the past two decades, and this farce was bringing a bad name to Indian cricket worldwide. N.S. Ramaswami condemned the act in his season summary in the *Indian Cricket*, calling it a craven surrender particularly considering Rajasthan had in their ranks such illustrious players.[43]

By the next season, the Ranji Trophy was for the first time divided into five zones—North, South, East, West and Central—in which Rajasthan topped the zone. They came up against eventual champions Baroda in the semi-final and this time it was Mankad as captain who conceded with a day to go after Rajasthan were forced to follow on. Durani did well with scores of 47 and 44 not out, but his bowling was still being underutilized and at this stage of his career he was playing as a specialist batsman.

The BCCI had finally had enough of this farce. They introduced a rule from the next season banning for two seasons

---

[43]Ramaswami, N.S., 'Notes on the Season 1956–56: Bombay Retain Championship', *Indian Cricket for 1956–57*, S.K. Gurunathan (ed.), Kasturi & Sons (Private) Ltd, Madras, 1958, pp. 82-85.

any team that conceded. N.S. Ramaswami heaved a sigh of relief in the next edition of the *Indian Cricket*!

The most infamous case of conceding denied an Indian player a prestigious world record. Nimbalkar is still the only Indian to score a first-class quadruple century even though he never played a Test match. Maharashtra ran up a massive 826 for four in reply to Kathiawar's 238. By lunch on the third day, Nimbalkar was batting on 443, just 10 runs short of beating Australian legend Donald Bradman's world record score of 452 not out scored in a Sheffield Shield match in Sydney in 1930.

During the break, Kathiawar captain Pradyumanshinhji, the Thakore Saheb of Rajkot, gave an ultimatum to his counterpart Yeshwant Gokhale to declare or he would concede—the result was a foregone conclusion after all. Gokhale pleaded for just another 10 minutes to enable the world record to pass into a fellow Indian's hands. But the Thakore Saheb refused and led his team off at lunch on the penultimate day of the four-day match since he claimed Maharashtra were only interested in playing for records.[44]

By 1958–59, when West Indies visited India for a five-Test series (which they won 3–0), Durani was in the reckoning for national honours. The home side was in shambles. The batting crumbled under a bouncer barrage unleashed by the fearsome Roy Gilchrist and Wes Hall, while the batsmen led by new world record holder (with 365 not out) Garry Sobers played merry with the Indian bowling. To top it all, India fielded four different captains in the five Tests.

Durani had his first opportunity to impress against the formidable visitors but did not do much with either bat or ball

---

[44]Ezekiel, Gulu, *Myths and Mysteries: Indian Sport Behind the Headlines*, Rupa Publications, New Delhi, 2023, p. 196.

for Board President's XI in the tour match at Ahmedabad before the first Test.

The first Test at Bombay ended in a draw and Durani got a second chance for Central Zone at Jabalpur. This time he came good with a sparkling 80 and was involved in a century partnership with Mankad (88). But it was not enough to force himself into the Test side. From this match, and for the rest of the domestic season, he was forced into keeping wickets as Rajasthan's regular keeper Sopan Sardesai had played his last match for them the previous season and they were without a ready replacement.

Wicketkeeping was in the genes but it was a role he was never comfortable in. It also meant his bowling would get neglected, a useful second bow to his string in his attempt to break into the Test side. Fortunately for Durani, Rajasthan and India, he was relieved of the burden by the 1959–60 season.

In 1958–59, Rajasthan fell once again at the semi-final stage. They were beaten by Bengal by nine wickets. Durani top scored with a watchful 66 in Rajasthan's first innings. In the last Central Zone league match, he got a long-awaited century against Vidarbha at Indore, only his second since his debut five years earlier. In fact, his 137 not out turned out to be the highest score of his career which included 14 centuries. It was his best season yet with the bat, 220 runs with an average of 55.

There was a bizarre situation in the first zonal match against Uttar Pradesh at Kanpur, in which Durani played a part behind the stumps. Uttar Pradesh, after following on 186 runs behind, were playing with dead bats to try to force the draw. Of the 97 overs bowled by Rajasthan in the innings, 33 produced just six runs. Now Rajasthan decided on a novel ploy to claim the new ball which, back then in India, was due at 150 runs in three-day matches—they kept bowling wide off the stumps, with Durani deliberately conceding boundary byes after boundary byes.

Rajasthan were desperate to claim the new ball even as time was running out. The spinners were being blocked by C.S. Nayudu and Ashwini Chaturvedi even as they added 81 runs for the sixth wicket in a crawl. Once the new ball was claimed, pace bowlers Arjun Naidu and Raj Singh, with nine wickets between them, scythed through the batting with the final wicket falling with just 10 minutes left in the match. Chaturvedi was caught by Durani off Raj Singh for 45 at 151 for six and the wickets then tumbled to leave UP 164 all out. Durani excelled with three brilliant catches and Rajasthan were home and dry by an innings and 22 runs.

Durani was disheartened when he was not picked in the touring party to England in 1959 despite batting consistently for Rajasthan. The tour, though, proved to be a disaster for Indian cricket as, for the first time, they were whitewashed in a series losing all five Tests. Whether Durani would have made a difference to the end result or not is debatable. But a possible mitigating factor was his lack of bowling in the 1958–59 season due to his wicket-keeping duties—that would have made him an added asset in England. It is likely that he missed out on selection for the national side in a sacrifice for his state side.

Finally, the chance came under fortuitous circumstances when Richie Benaud captained the second official Australian team that came to India in 1959–60 for five well-fought Test matches. Durani did reasonably well in the tour match for the Board President's XI at Ahmedabad with scores of 21 and 31.

I called Durani 'Destiny's Child' in the introduction. How he got a place in the India XI for the fourth Test at Bombay is one of those twists of fate in his charmed career that earns him that sobriquet.

After the 3–0 defeat at home at the hands of West Indies in 1958–59, and the whitewash in England in 1959, Indian cricket was going through one of its periodical low ebbs. The mighty

Australians were coming to India after winning two of the three Tests in Pakistan. They had also crushed South Africa 3–0 and England 4–0 in the Ashes in previous seasons and could make a claim to being the unofficial world champions. Further, coming into this series, Benaud as captain had won six of his eight Tests and not lost once.

Only her most ardent fans would have given India a ghost of a chance of avoiding another drubbing. As chairman of the selection committee, Lala Amarnath's first task was to remove D.K. Gaekwad, who had captained the disastrous tour in England. His choice of the 32-year-old G.S. Ramchand proved to be a masterstroke, and not his last in the series either.

Benaud was determined to keep his slate clean as captain. While things did not turn out that way, the series started predictably enough. Australia romped to victory by an innings in the first Test in Delhi and panic began to set in the Indian camp. It was India's fifth innings defeat in a miserable year and the ninth defeat in their last 11 Tests. That the team would face yet another whitewash was the fear.

India just had a couple of days to recoup for the Kanpur Test. Changes had to be made and off spinner/batsman A.G. Kripal Singh and off spinner Jasubhai Patel were brought in. But only one would play in the XI.

The Kanpur Miracle

Patel's previous Test was three years ago and his record was distinctly ordinary. He just had four Tests to his credit in a span of four years in which he had taken 10 wickets. The news of selection came as a shock to all cricket fans and even to the 35-year-old Patel himself.

His young daughter opened the newspaper on a chilly December morning in Ahmedabad and broke the news to her stunned father that he was among the 15 for the Kanpur Test. He could scarcely believe his ears. Patel, in fact, was in a dilemma whether to go to Kanpur or not.

'I was not in practice. I had lost all hopes of playing in Tests,' he told C.N. Venugopal.[45]

Reluctantly, he travelled to Kanpur, convinced that the selectors would prefer Kripal, a batsman with a century on his Test debut four years earlier and a useful off spinner to boot.

The next morning though, Amarnath—who brooked no answer in Indian cricket back then—made the shocking announcement. The specialist off spinner would be in the playing XI.

So what was the thinking behind this huge gamble? According to his youngest son, Rajendar Amarnath, 'Amarnath reached Kanpur a day before the Test and saw some loose spots at the good length spot. Knowing the Australian's weakness against off spin, he wanted Jasu Patel to play.'[46] But he needed Ramchand's concurrence for his choice. The captain was non-committal. But Amarnath used his powers of persuasion and Patel was in.

By the close of the first day, it looked like another big defeat was on the cards. The Indian batting crumbled to 152 all out, nine of the 10 wickets falling to spin. Famed left-arm fast bowler Alan Davidson, realizing he would get no assistance from the track, turned to spin and grabbed five wickets. Ramchand winning the toss would prove vital on this pitch that was already crumbling on the very first day.

By the second day, Australia looked well-set for a big lead going into lunch on 128 for one. Patel was in despair, so was Amarnath. Would his gamble misfire? The bowler had been

---

[45]Venugopal, C.N., 'Tale of Reluctant Hero of Kanpur', *The Times of India*, 6 April 1969.

[46]Amarnath, Rajendar, *The Making of a Legend: Lala Amarnath: Life & Times*, Rupa Publications, New Delhi, 2004, p. 227.

pleading with his reluctant captain to let him change bowling ends, but to no avail. But at the break it was once again Amarnath's persuasion that did the trick.

Off the very first ball after the break, Patel bowled Colin McDonald (53) having earlier claimed the wicket of the other opener, Gavin Stevens. The rout was now on. The next eight wickets collapsed for the addition of 91 runs, with Neil Harvey's half-century the only modicum of resistance. Australia were all out for 219. Seven of those eight wickets fell to Patel who now had the chance to exploit the footmarks left by Davidson and fast bowler Ian Meckiff, an off spinner's specialty.

Patel finished with the astonishing figures of 35.5-16-69-9, including a magical spell of eight for 24. Leg spinner Chandu Borde claimed the lone wicket not taken by Patel—that of Norman O'Neill. Just one season earlier, leg spinner Subhash Gupte had taken nine for 102 against West Indies at the same venue. Patel improved on that and it would remain the best Test bowling figures by an Indian till Anil Kumble's 10 for 74 against Pakistan at New Delhi in 1999.

Australia still had a first innings lead of 67 runs and the onus was now on the Indian batsmen to come good in the second innings, a feat they performed well, and the total of 291 meant Australia were set a target of 225 runs in order to record their second straight win in the series.

It was never on. Patel's five wickets were augmented by Polly Umrigar's four as Australia fell in a heap for 105. All the Aussie wickets in both innings fell to spinners, and India were triumphant by 119 runs. Patel's 14 for 124 were the best Test match bowling figures for India till leg spinner Narendra Hirwani's 16 for 136 on debut against West Indies at Madras in 1988.

To say the country went gaga with joy would not be an exaggeration. Congratulations poured in, including those from the president and prime minister. It was as if a huge burden had been lifted off the shoulders of Indian cricket, which had staggered from one crisis to another throughout the past 12 months. Even the normally staid *The Hindu* splashed the news on their front page, complete with photos of the victorious XI.

It was India's sixth Test victory since their first against England in Madras in 1952. But the previous five had come against a second-string English side as well as Pakistan and New Zealand who, along with India, were considered to be the minnows of Test cricket back then. This one was against a full-strength Aussie team packed with all-time greats like Benaud, Harvey, Davidson and O'Neill. It was surely Indian cricket's finest hour.

The Aussies were neither happy with the Green Park pitch nor with Patel's action, which had a cloud of suspicion over its legality. But the captain and his troops kept their silence as it had been dinned into them that the tours to both Pakistan and India had a diplomatic angle as well to them.

It was thus with a heady feeling of relief and joy that the Indian team moved on to Bombay for the third Test at Brabourne Stadium starting on New Year's Day in 1960. And then came the twist of fate connecting Patel and Durani. It may be recalled here that Patel, as the captain of Gujarat, had persuaded Durani to switch teams from Saurashtra. When, two seasons later, Durani decided to make the move to Rajasthan, Patel tried his best to dissuade him.

Poor Patel hardly had any time to savour the Kanpur victory. Just days later, he was back home in Ahmedabad where he was captaining the Board President's XI against the tourists. It was in Ahmedabad that he reportedly fell ill with food poisoning. He missed the Test at Bombay that immediately followed Kanpur. Did he miss this vital Test for health reasons or because the typically flat Brabourne pitch would not suit him and would allow the Aussie batsmen to get on top of his bowling? This, too, was a theory floated at the time for his surprising exclusion. Or was it something more sinister?

Amarnath, for his part, was playing his cards close to his chest. He initially released only 10 names for Bombay as he was awaiting the conclusion of the Ahmedabad tour game in which Durani scored 21 and 31. The Bombay Test began three days after the end of the tour game and, while Patel was present in Bombay, he did not play after all, though he was back for the fourth Test at Madras and the fifth and final at Calcutta.

Benaud took at dig at Patel in his book, noting his rapid recovery from his apparent illness. 'Jasu Patel had become perfectly fit [for the Madras Test] very quickly having missed the Bombay match [...]'[47] Was Benaud holding back something? The cryptic sentence appears to indicate so. So what was the story behind this episode?

The late journalist Raju Bharathan was reporting the Test match. He asked captain Ramchand how come Patel did not play in Bombay? 'Is it true, Ram, that you chose to "hide" Jasu Patel from the Aussies on that Brabourne Stadium featherbed?' 'Nonsense!' came back Ramchand. 'Patel did not play in that key third Test simply because he himself shied away from that game, apprehensive of being no-balled for "throwing" by that very strict umpire ND Nagarwala.'[48]

Nagarwala, best known for being the coach of Chandu Borde, was an accomplished all-round sportsman from Poona. Unusually for Indian umpires of that era, he was also a former first-class cricketer. This incidentally was the fifth and final Test of his umpiring career. He had a reputation on the domestic circuit for calling out bowlers with dodgy actions and Patel's

---

[47]Benaud, Richie, *Anything but...An Autobiography*, Hodder & Staughton, Great Britain, 1999, p. 170.

[48]Raju Bharathan, 'Another test of strength altogether', *The Hindu*, 7 March 1998.

was certainly not above board. Another Bombay debutant was Budhi Kunderan, the dashing wicketkeeper batsman. He and Durani through the sixties would go a long way in erasing the 'dull dogs' tag Indian cricketers had earned in the 1950s.

While Durani could thank a stroke of fortune for his Test debut, it was sheer bad luck that he should injure a finger on his bowling hand during a practice session. As a result, he was pushed down to number 10 in the first innings and bowled just one over in the Australian second innings that lasted less than half an hour.

He told Rameshwar Singh that he was chatting with Kunderan and Man Mohan Sood on the eve of the Test when Mohammad, a waiter at the Cricket Club of India (CCI), Brabourne Stadium, came and told him, 'Lala Amarnath sahib *bula rahe hain.*' ('Lala Amarnath is calling you.') He was the chief selector, so Budhi said, 'Salim, *lagta hai teri lottery lag gayi.*' ('It looks like you have won the lottery.')[49]

On being told by Amarnath that he was playing, Salim ran to Ramchand's room and said, 'Skip, can I borrow your India blazer? I want to get a photo clicked.'[50] Ramchand gave him his blazer which was loose for him, but he still got the photo taken and it remained his proud possession.

Understandably, he could not sleep the night before the Test with excitement. Surely the news would have reached his proud father across the border too.

Test Debut

And so, 10 years after he made his first appearance at a national-level event, Salim Durani, at 26 years of age, had finally

---

[49]Text from Rameshwar Singh to author dated 26 May 2023.
[50]Ibid.

reached the pinnacle of any cricketer's ambition—to wear the country's colours.

India's first innings of 289 was marked by Nari Contractor's lone Test century and 50 by the Oxford undergraduate Abbas Ali Baig, who had been flown out from England specially for the first three Tests before going back to resume his studies. His century on his Test debut six months earlier at Old Trafford was one of the few bright spots in India's dismal 1959 tour and was the first such instance by an Indian abroad.

Durani's 18 took an hour, he played in an unusually defensive manner. But then he had the injury to contend with. He also said, 'I have never played a subdued game. That was my first Test and I was naturally apprehensive [...] I hated bowlers dominating me.'[51] Though he batted just once in the Test since India declared at 226 for five in the second innings, his brief knock gave him confidence as he faced bowlers of the calibre of Benaud, Davidson, Ray Lindwall and Ian Meckiff, before he was caught by Stevens off Benaud.

Australia had gained a near-100 run lead. After an opening stand worth 95 between Pankaj Roy and Contractor in the second innings, Australia were sniffing victory when wickets fell in a heap and the scoreboard suddenly read 112 for four, a lead of just 14 runs. That's when Ramnath Kenny and Baig, with his second half-century of the Test, got together with their rescue act to make things safe for India and salvage an honourable draw.

There was an amusing incident as the two batsmen walked off for tea on the final day. A young lady in a skirt ran onto the field and planted a kiss on the blushing Baig's cheek. The crowd roared with delight and the incident became a part of Indian cricket's folklore and popular culture. Three of the cricketers I mentioned in my introduction who were part of the glamorous

---

[51]Memon, Ayaz, 'Mr Sixer', *Cricketer Asia*, July 1983.

era of the 1960s were playing in this Test—Baig, Kunderan and Durani.

When I spoke to Baig on 10 June 2023 and asked him about his memories of the Test and especially of Durani's debut, he said he had no memories as such about the match. When I reminded him about the kiss, he laughed and said, 'Yes, how can anyone forget that?'[52]

As for his teammate, Baig told me, 'Salim was an excellent all-rounder who would be an asset to any domestic or international side. He was an exciting stroke-player and as a bowler had a lovely high arm action. As a person, Salim was a fun-loving personality and a good singer too.'

Unusually, it was Durani's fielding that came in for high praise in contemporary reports, an aspect of this dazzling all-rounder's skill set that would let him down in later years.

With Patel now fit, Durani was made twelfth man for the next Test at Madras and dropped altogether for the fifth and final at Calcutta, one of those inexplicable acts Indian selectors were notorious for. Australia won by an innings at Madras while the Calcutta Test was drawn. Both sides would have been satisfied with the final 2-1 scoreline—Australia returned with their honour intact after the Kanpur humiliation, while India would have been relieved having held their own against the mighty Aussies.

Patel, with just five wickets from those last two Tests, never played for India again—finishing his career with 27 wickets from seven Tests—and slipped back into the relative obscurity of the Ranji Trophy. A one-Test wonder if ever there was one. Imagine his delight then, when he and former captain Vijay Hazare, became the first cricketers to be awarded the Padma Shri. In Sujit Mukherjee's memorable description, 'The great

---

[52]Ezekiel, Gulu, *Myth-Busting: Indian Cricket Behind the Headlines*, Rupa Publications, New Delhi, 2021, p. 194.

performance was recognized by the Government of India in the shape of a "Padma Shri" award in 1960 to Jasu M. Patel who looked as bewildered during the investiture ceremony at Delhi as he had while he was whisking Australians out in processional order in Kanpur.'[53]

Over to England

Having never experienced alien cricket conditions in his life, Durani now decided to try his hand at club cricket in England during the summer of 1960 on the advice of Maharana Bhagwat Singh. It was a whole new world for him as well as a fresh source of revenue, and he would be walking among the giants of the game to boot.

Before the English counties opened up to professionals from around the world in 1968, it was the various leagues across England, particularly the Lancashire Leagues, that attracted the cream of cricketers worldwide for lucrative contracts.

Every cricket country in the world was represented with legends like the West Indians Frank Worrell, Wes Hall and Garry Sobers, among others. As for Indians, famed fast bowler L. Amar Singh was among the first to go in the 1930s. Big names like Amarnath, Mankad, Dattu Phadkar, Gupte and Manjrekar down to the more recent V.V.S. Laxman, Manoj Prabhakar, Vinod Kambli and others spent their summers playing club cricket in England. Even post-1968, many famous players continued to play in the leagues—AB de Villiers, Viv Richards, Wasim Akram, Dean Jones, Steve Smith—the list goes on.

The workload was light—matches on the weekend and coaching in the evenings through the rest of the week. Some

---

[53]Mukherjee, Sujit, *Playing for India*, Orient Longman Limited, Madras, 1972, p. 213.

even allowed their players to be guest players for other clubs. The players were usually put up with local families and forged close ties with the community, which embraced them with open arms. For players from abroad, the strength of the pound sterling against their local currencies was a big incentive—useful money during their off-seasons. The IPL has of course changed this scenario, as it has so much else in the cricket world. But the leagues continue to hold their own.

It should be noted here that these matches are not considered first-class and hence are not part of the official records of the participants. That did not, however, deter the hundreds who made their living there over the decades. Sir Garfield Sobers, the greatest all-rounder in cricketing history, played cricket the year round as a full-time professional for two decades in England even while turning out for West Indies in Test cricket and in their domestic championship.

Apart from the annual fee, there was also the tradition of the 'whip around', where a player who scored a 50 or took five wickets in an innings could earn a bit extra as a collection was made from the crowd, spectators chipping in with a shilling or two.

These collections helped the pros earn extra and was also an incentive to excel. Worrell, Sobers' mentor who was an old hand in the leagues, taught his protégé a trick or two—when you reach your fifty, he had told the young Garry, don't give away your wicket, look around the boundary, take note of the richer fans, who would be more generous with their donations, and make sure the collection box passed by them before you get out. Such was the life of the cricket professional back then—even if that professional happened to be one of the greatest cricketers who ever lived.

Today, the proliferation of T20 franchise leagues around the world, the IPL by far being the most lucrative, means many cricketers are walking away from international cricket to become freelance professionals, flying around the world to appear in leagues across the globe.

Those who continue to represent their country risk injury and burnout in these leagues and often turn up the night before a Test match without proper preparation or acclimatization. Tours today have become truncated, with warm-up games a thing of the past, as internationals are packed close together to give more time for players to ply their trade in the T20 leagues.

And as much as cricket purists today like to bemoan this 'commercialization', it was just the same with the English leagues as well as county cricket, which often paid substantially more than national duty.

In a despairing analysis in the February 1962 issue of *Playfair Cricket Monthly*, John Kay wrote under the heading 'Club or Country—Trouble Brewing' that the West Indians Conrad Hunte, Wes Hall, Seymour Nurse and Chester Watson were liable to miss the last two Tests of the Indians' series in West Indies as they were contracted to clubs in the Lancashire League and there would be a clash of dates with the start of the English season. Chandu Borde, who was with Rawtenstall, was also named. In the case of Sobers and Radcliffe, the West Indies board agreed to pay the fees of a replacement till Sobers could rejoin the club at the end of the Test series. The BCCI had agreed to their tour late and this upset the schedules of the English clubs.[54]

Eventually, the players mentioned were allowed to take part in the Test series. But Kay claimed the league clubs felt that they were 'being taken for a ride' by several big-name players 'and this may result in a showdown of major proportions'. After

---

[54]Kay, John, 'Club or Country–Trouble Brewing', *Playfair Cricket Monthly*, February 1962.

all, the clubs were shelling out big bucks for their contracted players, far more than what they earned playing Tests.

Sounds familiar? It should!

Perhaps the most famous (or infamous) example of this old-style club versus country clash came when India were to tour England in 1952. Vinoo Mankad, then the leading all-rounder in the world, had just received a lucrative offer from Haslingden in the Lancashire League. In November 1951, he requested the BCCI for a guarantee that he would be selected for the tour of England so that he could respond to the club's offer. The Board snubbed his request and, to add salt to the wound, the chairman of the selectors, C.K. Nayudu, made a disparaging remark about him that Mankad never forgave him for.

The result was a disaster. In the first Test at Headingley, Leeds, India came up against a ferocious fast bowler making his Test debut on his home turf. Fred Trueman would one day become the first bowler in history to reach 300 Test wickets. And on his debut, all the other players and the spectators at the ground could only look on in shock as the 2nd innings' scoreboard showed India zero for four—Trueman taking three of those wickets—an unheard-of start in the history of Test cricket. Though there was something of a recovery, the defeat by seven wickets was a humiliating one for India.

The touring team management pressed the panic button. Frantic cables flew to and from England and India. The plea was for the selectors to eat humble pie and call up Mankad from the leagues. This they did at great cost and the very next Test at Lord's went into the history books as 'Mankad's Match'—a phenomenal all-round performance of 72 and 184 and five for 196 from 73 overs in England's first innings. Even though this Test too was lost, Indian cricket's honour had been saved by one man.

Durani represented Stockport in the Central Lancashire League in 1960, the same year Sobers did the 'double' for the first time for Radcliffe, finishing the season with 1,113 runs at 48.39 and exactly 100 wickets at 10.37. Three other bowlers took 100 or more wickets for the season but none could match Sobers' all-round feat. As was expected, it was Mankad who preceded Durani at Stockport in 1959, and recommended the latter to the club for the next year.

Durani's record was somewhat modest but good enough considering this was his first taste of cricket outside India. He scored 790 runs at 31.60 and claimed 68 wickets with his left-arm spin at 16.04. But he did not return in 1961 as he did not agree to Stockport's offer of £450. He was replaced by the West Indian Test all-rounder Reg Scarlett. He did not return in 1962 either.

Instead, in those two years, he deputized for Mankad at Tonge in the Bolton Cricket League. He was not a contracted professional, but would have received payment for the matches in which he took the place of Mankad and stayed with his guru and father figure during those two seasons. Vinoo, his wife and three sons, all accepted Salim as one of their own.

However, Durani did return to England for a full season in 1963, when he was contracted to Great Chell in the North Staffordshire and South Cheshire League, and this time he commanded a handsome fee of £750 thanks to his outstanding performance against the touring English side in 1961–62.

Durani was eighth in the batting averages with 611 runs from 20 innings at 33.94. He was tenth in the bowling averages with 64 wickets at 13.07. Only the Australian bowler Cec Pepper took more wickets than him. Garry's elder brother, Gerry Sobers, substituted for him at Norton since Garry was part of the West Indies touring team that year under Worrell's captaincy. Durani's best performance came against Knypersley, scoring 63 runs and capturing eight wickets for 77 runs.

Durani was also contracted to coach and a report in The

Cricketer mentions this. 'Great Chell are banking on the coaching of Salim Durani to build up their playing fortunes, but he is proving a capable player also, as witness his figures against Crewe LMR—32 runs and five for 71.'[55]

The professional before him in 1961 at the club was the South African all-rounder Trevor Goddard, and after him in 1964 it was the great West Indian fast bowler Wes Hall.

How Great Chell got in touch with Durani and how they recruited him was revealed to me through the minutes of the meetings of the club held in December 1962. These were provided to me via email in June 2023 by Stephen Goold, whose father Graham was on the club committee at the time. They make for interesting reading.[56]

According to the meeting held on 14 December 1962, a letter was sent to Durani asking if he would be interested in signing with the club. Since his address was not known, it was sent to the BCCI requesting them to forward it to Durani. A reply was received from Durani from Madras where he was residing at the time, confirming his interest for a fee of £750 'with permission to coach boys.'[57]

Following the reply, a further letter was sent to Durani asking for more details and also to Stockport Cricket Club asking them for details of Durani's performance and conduct when he played for them in 1960. What apparently clinched the deal was when the chairman of the club obtained copies of *The Cricketer* detailing Durani's excellent performance against

---

[55] *The Cricketer*, 7 June 1963.
[56] I am indebted to Scott Oliver, author of *Sticky Dogs and Stardust: When Cricket's Legends Played in the League*, for his excellent knowledge of the leagues and contacts and to my friend Marcus Lee—who played in the Bradford League—for his invaluable inputs. The details of Durani's English league exploits are being published here for the first time.
[57] Ibid.

the English touring team in the 1961–62 series.

'These details were read to the Committee from which it was seen that Durani put up very good performances both with the bat and ball, particularly the fifth Test match in which Durani and Borde were largely responsible between them for India winning this match.'[58]

Durani signed the contract on 2 January 1963.

Of course, news travelled slowly back then. But it is also clear from the minutes that the committee were unaware of the details of England's tour of India the previous winter. Detailed reports from correspondents on tour were only available in the dailies when England took on Australia, South Africa and West Indies, considered the major Test teams. A tour of India, Pakistan and New Zealand would barely get a mention in the press.

And so Durani's grand performance in his first full Test series saw his fee jump from £450, which he turned down in 1961, to £750 two years later, a very generous amount for the time, an amount that he gladly accepted. As a bonus, his cricket knowledge and experience got a boost by playing outside India.

---

[58]Ibid.

Three

Golden Run (1960–61 to 1964–65)

Salim Durani's bowling, which had been neglected early on in his career, came into its own in the early 1960s. It proved an asset to both Durani and his teams—Rajasthan, Central Zone, Rest of India and India. To be considered a genuine all-rounder and to enhance his worth to his teams, it was essential that this skill not be neglected or, indeed, shelved.

At the junior level, his left-arm spin was very much part of his all-round armoury and that is how he first made his mark on the national scene. But as he broke into first-class cricket in 1953–54, it tended to be neglected by his captains and perhaps by Salim himself as his batting blossomed. In one season (1958–59) it was completely forgotten as he was forced to don the wicketkeeper's gloves in the Ranji Trophy since Rajasthan were without a regular wicketkeeper.

Durani's final Test figures—1,202 runs at 25.04 with one century and seven fifties and 75 wickets at 35.42, three times five wickets in an innings and once 10 in a match—make it hard to categorize him as either a batting or a bowling all-rounder. Perhaps it is best to say he was a bit of both. His first-class figures—8,545 runs at 33.37 and 484 wickets at 26.09—veer slightly towards the former. But what is clear is that, at his best, he was a match-winner with both bat or ball, and often both in the same match. Durani himself was proud of his bowling skills which he learned from an all-time master, Vinoo Mankad.

So what kind of bowler was he? In his own words, 'I could spin the ball anywhere; I used a lot of change of pace; I used to release the ball in a variety of ways; my arm ball would hustle off the pitch [...]'[59]

Having been consigned to the backwaters of domestic cricket after just that one Test match in the 1959–60 series against Australia, Durani was now able to fully concentrate on Rajasthan's fortunes in the Ranji Trophy. Pakistan were in India in 1960–61 for five Tests, all of which ended in dreary draws. Durani was in the reserves but he did get one chance to play against the tourists. It was for Central Zone at Nagpur and, while he failed to impress, he had the opportunity to meet Hanif Mohammad's kid brother Mushtaq Mohammad, who at 15-years-old the previous year was the youngest Test cricketer when he made his debut against West Indies.

Hanif, who by that time was one of the world's leading batsmen, was rested for the match that was played between the first Test at Bombay and the second at Kanpur. Mushtaq and Salim spent time together, with Salim no doubt curious to know about the father who had left the family behind in 1947 and who had not met his wife and children again since. 'I had a great regard for him [Salim], and he was like a family member,' Mushtaq was quoted as saying.[60]

When I texted Mushtaq, now residing in England, about the meeting, he told me, 'Master Aziz was not the cricket coach only to Hanif Mohammed and many other young cricketers, he was more than that, he was very close to Hanif bhai. And

---

[59]Giridhar, S., and V.J. Raghunath, *Mid-Wicket Tales: From Trumper to Tendulkar*, Sage Publications, New Delhi, 2014, p. 35.
[60]Heller, Richard, and Peter Oborne, *White on Green: Celebrating the Drama of Pakistan Cricket*, Simon & Schuster, London, 2016, p. 89.

one could say, Hanif Mohammed was the product of Master Aziz. He will be always remembered.'

Mushtaq, however, would not be drawn into what the conversation was like between him and Salim. Or maybe he had no recollection of the same—after all, it had been 63 years since the two met.[61]

Even 20 years later, Durani's exclusion from the series rankled as he said in an interview in 1979. When asked by Raju Bharatan if he felt he should have been included in the team, he replied, 'The hell I should have! I had done very well in the Ranji Trophy matches preceding the arrival of Fazal Mahmood and his men in India. I would have changed the entire tenure of the [dull] series! Remember, I was young and full of go [...] Twenty years they wouldn't let me hit Pak for six.'[62]

While his bowling was outstanding in the 1960–61 season with 35 wickets in five matches in the Ranji Trophy, averaging 10.94, his batting was a disappointment—133 runs at 22.16 with just one half-century.

Rajasthan's Year

Since he was in the reserves of the national team for most of the 1959–60 season, Durani was only available for Rajasthan in the losing quarter-final against Services. Fortunately, they had obtained the services of another accomplished left-handed all-rounder, the Test player Rusi Surti from Gujarat, who could bowl both pace and spin. But it had been a disappointing season under the captaincy of Mankad. Perhaps the burden was too heavy on the veteran master who was in the twilight of his glittering career.

---

[61]Text exchange between Mushtaq Mohammad and the author on 13 June 2023.
[62]Bharatan, Raju, 'Wish They Had Let Me Hit Pak for Six!', *The Illustrated Weekly of India*, Sunday, 25 November, 1979.

Mankad was replaced as captain by Kishan Rungta for 1960–61—though Mankad remained an integral part of the side—and there was an immediate change of fortunes. The addition of legendary leg spinner Subhash Gupte from Bombay added considerable sting to the bowling.

For the first time, Rajasthan made it to the Ranji Trophy final. Durani did the star turn with both bat and ball in the first Central Zone match against Uttar Pradesh. Uttar Pradesh were all out for 229. But when Vijay Manjrekar (33) was third out at 97, Rajasthan were in a spot of bother. This is where the mentor (Mankad 127) and disciple (Durani 57) pulled off the rescue act with a stand worth 110 at quicker than a run a minute.

Pushing for an outright win, Rungta declared at 296 for nine. Now Durani was simply unplayable as his analysis of 13-2-20-5 shows; UP were 132 all out. It was the first five-wicket haul of his career and helped Rajasthan romp to victory by seven wickets. He was devastating with the ball again as Vidarbha were crushed by an innings in Nagpur in the next game. His figures of five for 37 and four for 34 gave him a match haul of nine for 71, his best to date.

With six wickets in his next match, Durani was proving to be Rajasthan's trump card as they raced to their third straight win, beating Madhya Pradesh by nine wickets to easily top the Central Zone points table. He now had 21 wickets from the league stage, and Rajasthan were riding the crest of a wave going into the semi-finals.

They came up against Madras at their home ground, the Corporation Stadium (later Nehru Stadium), and it was a grim battle of wits over four days of pulsating cricket. Rajasthan took first strike on winning the toss. They were struggling after losing their top five batsmen for 125 runs with medium pacer U. Prabhakar Rao grabbing four. Mankad, Bhagwat Singh, Manjrekar and Durani were all dismissed cheaply with only Surti (59) keeping the bowlers at bay.

Now Hanumant and skipper Rungta began the recovery, their sixth wicket partnership almost doubling the total. Rungta, who top scored for Rajasthan with 74, had an escape on 21 when he was dropped by leg spinner V.V. Kumar off his own bowling. In retrospect, that could be seen as the turning point of the entire match. The stand was worth 117 in 108 minutes before Rungta was run out. After that, Hanumant's elder brother and wicketkeeper Suryaveer Singh chipped in with useful runs as Rajasthan, overnight 283 for six, reached 301.

The battle for the vital first innings lead was a tense affair. Madras lost their first five wickets for 125, identical to Rajasthan, with Durani claiming three of those, including the main wicket of Test player and captain C.D. Gopinath for 12. It was left to A.G. Milkha Singh, elder brother A.G. Kripal Singh and V. Sridhar, whose 98 was the highest score of the match, to stretch the total to 328, a lead of just 27 runs. Milkha was bowled by a peach of a delivery from Durani, the ball turning in viciously. The lead was eked out only after the fall of the eighth wicket. Durani, with three for 73 from 28 overs, out-bowled his more illustrious teammates, Gupte and Mankad, who had two wickets apiece.

With the pitch now wearing out and taking spin, the Madras bowlers, and in particular Kumar, were able to put a brake on Rajasthan's second innings even as they tried to get quick runs to force a decision. Twenty wickets fell in all on the fourth and final day, with all but three going to the spin bowlers. Rajasthan all out for 210 meant Madras needed a modest 184 for victory. It was not to be. Madras succumbed to Rajasthan's spin trio of Gupte, Mankad and Durani, who once again took three wickets to finish with six for the match. As in the first innings, he accounted for Gopinath whose 35 was the highest for Madras. He then mopped up the tail, finishing with three for six from 5.4 overs.

Madras all out for 116, Rajasthan storming back to victory by 67 runs and into the final with holders Bombay who crushed Delhi by an innings and 203 runs in the other semi-final, 'Bapu' Nadkarni scoring a monumental 283 not out.

Maharana Bhagwat Singh's dream of winning the Ranji Trophy was now one step closer to fruition. The final was held in his backyard, so to say, the Bhupal Nobles' College ground at Udaipur. It was to be played on an unused coir matting strip laid over a freshly made pitch. Bombay had won the title the two previous seasons and were hot favourites to make it a hat-trick under the captaincy of Polly Umrigar. Former Bombay captain and batting legend Vijay Merchant's report appeared in *The Indian Cricket-Field Annual* and he described a colourful scene at Udaipur with *shamianas* (awnings) all around the boundary. He was however critical of the outfield which he described as 'rough and stony'.[63]

Bombay ran away winners by seven wickets for their third title on the trot under the captaincy of Umrigar. But the real hero of the match was Durani who, in the first innings, bowled a lion-hearted spell, though it was all to be in vain. Rajasthan collapsed to 140, thus squandering the advantage of winning the toss. Ramakant Desai, nicknamed 'Tiny' for his short stature, was the quickest bowler in India at the time and had a giant heart in his tiny frame. Within the first hour of play, he silenced the partisan crowd by knocking over Mankad, Bhagwat and Surti with the total at just 37. He was able to extract disconcerting bounce from even the good length spot and Bombay already had their tails up. Ramchand then dismissed Durani for 12 and Desai came back to send back brothers Hanumant and Suryaveer,

---

[63]Merchant, Vijay, *The Indian Cricket-Field Annual 1961–62*, Dicky Rutnagur (ed.), Bombay, 1962, p. 261. The annual ran for seven editions from 1957–58 till 1964–65.

neither having scored. Only Manjrekar (40) and Rungta put up a modicum of a fight as Rajasthan folded up 70 minutes after lunch. Desai (seven for 46) was in devastating form.

Bombay, too, stumbled at the start, losing four wickets before reaching three figures. Three Test batsmen, Madhav Apte, Manohar Hardikar and Umrigar, all fell to Durani's guile. But Bombay's batting had enormous depth. Ramchand rode his luck to hit a rapid century, while Nadkarni fell just four runs short of his own. Durani got both of them but their 187-run partnership for the fifth wicket took the match away from Rajasthan. The total of 346 meant Bombay had gained a huge lead. And even though their opponents improved in the second innings, it was not enough to stop Bombay's charge to victory.

Merchant wrote of Durani's figures of 31.5-5-99-8, 'No praise could be too high for Durani, whose effort was every bit as great as Desai's, perhaps more creditable considering the opposition he encountered. Except when Ramchand and Nadkarni were at the wicket, Durani looked like he was splitting the Bombay batting wide open. He spun the ball viciously and put in so much of toil that his spinning finger got skinned and in the later stages of the innings, he bowled in great pain. But he was adequately rewarded for his gallantry, eight wickets falling to him for 99 runs. As one who is likely to produce great results on a wicket offering the slightest help, *the Indian selectors would do well to keep Durani in mind.*' [emphasis mine][64]

An added asset for Rajasthan in the 1960s was coach Nariman D. Marshall. The fiery-tempered Parsi was the first Indian instructor for cricket coaches at the National Institute of Sports, Patiala, before moving to Jaipur. He had been on the first official tour of England in 1932 as a batsman though he never played a Test. Durani's 35 wickets in the Ranji Trophy

---

[64]Ibid.

that season put him top of the charts, just one more than Desai. Now he had jumped to the front of the selectors' queue for a Test recall.

The only participant from that final still alive is Chandrakant Patankar, wicketkeeper and opening batsman. Dr Patankar, when I spoke to him for this book, was the third oldest living Indian Test cricketer (born 24 November 1930) after D.K. Gaekwad, who subsequently passed away in February 2024, and C.D. Gopinath. He also played against Rajasthan in the 1965–66 final at Jaipur and represented India in a lone Test match against New Zealand at Calcutta in 1955–56, in which he had three catches and one stumping. Understandably, at 93, Dr Patankar had no memories of a match that was played over 60 years ago. But he did recall that the captain in that 1960–61 final was Umrigar and in 1965–66 it was Nadkarni. Umrigar, he said, was the best as he 'led from the front' being an excellent all-rounder.[65]

So what made Bombay tick all those years? Patankar puts it down to the rich talent the side had with eight or nine Test cricketers of the calibre of Umrigar, Nadkarni, Sardesai, Desai, Ramchand, Subhash and Baloo Gupte, among others. 'Other teams had just one of two big names,' he told me. 'Maharashtra had Chandu Borde, Baroda had Vijay Hazare. Rajasthan had the services of Manjrekar, Gupte, Durani and others and were a good side but they never stood a chance against Bombay,' he said with a chuckle.[66]

'What made us special is we were *khadoos* cricketers.' That Marathi word denotes a never-say-die attitude. It has often been used to describe what set the Bombay team apart from the rest and saw them win the Ranji Trophy 15 years on the trot from

---

[65]Conversation with the author on 18 June 2023.
[66]Ibid.

1958–59 to 1972–73 and 41 times in all, an extraordinary feat not replicated in domestic cricket anywhere else in the world. 'When teams would come up against Bombay they would suffer from an inferiority complex, a lack of confidence. And cricket is after all a game of confidence. Look at Maharashtra. They would do well against all other teams but when it came to Bombay only Borde would do well.'[67]

Although he did not have a clear recollection of Durani's brilliant bowling in the 1960–61 final, he felt he was 'moody and temperamental, a happy-go-lucky cricketer who would love playing to the galleries.' Durani, Dr Patankar said, was a fine all-rounder and always good company but he did not take his cricket as seriously as some of the Bombay players back then. 'Still he should have played more Tests than he did.'[68]

Durani on the back of his bowling achievements that season was chosen as one of the *Indian Cricket*'s Five Cricketers of the Year in their 1960–61 edition. This is how L.N. Mathur summed him up in his profile, 'The coming years are crucial in Salim's cricketing career. He is lucky to be employed on the personal staff of the Maharaja of Mewar, one of the greatest patrons of cricket. In such favourable atmosphere if he makes the best use of his talent Salim will go a long way in cricket.'[69]

The First Comeback

The BCCI made a positive move by introducing the Duleep Trophy for the five zones in the 1961–62 season. It gave first-class cricketers another opportunity to catch the selectors' eye apart from the Ranji Trophy where they could play just

---
[67]Ibid.
[68]Ibid.
[69]Mathur, L.N., *Indian Cricket for 1960–61*, S.K. Gurunathan (ed.), Kasturi & Sons Limited, Madras, 1961, p. 30.

a handful of matches. In 1945–46, a similar tournament was introduced, the Zonal Quadrangular, but it lasted just two seasons. That though was for four zones—North, South, East and West—and did not include Central. Now players from the Central Zone would get an added opportunity, too.

With Rajasthan's Ranji campaign kicking off as late as December 1961, and with England returning to India for a series for the first time in 10 years, it was in the Duleep Trophy in September that Durani got his chance to further his claims for a Test spot. He was an outstanding success, both in batting and bowling. 'Durani burst forth with a new brilliance in the tournament,'[70] was how *Indian Cricket* annual in its 1962 edition described his performance. His 244 runs from two matches was the highest total in the inaugural tournament. He hit 78 in Central's first match against East which was won on spin of the coin with rain curtailing the first innings.

In the second match, Central versus West at Baroda, he scored a sparkling century in the first innings and 56 in the second against the strongest bowling attack in the country consisting of Desai, Nadkarni, Surti and Borde. To top it all, he claimed three wickets in West's first innings, including that of century-maker Borde. But he could not prevent West winning before going on to beat South in the inaugural final in Bombay.

That Central/West semi-final was a thriller till the first innings. Both Durani and Manjrekar scored centuries and their partnership worth 205 runs for the third wicket helped Central to 330. Durani had two 'lives' but so effortless was his batting that his inclusion in the Indian side for the first Test against the English tourists was now a given. The series was to start just a month after the Duleep final.

It was not till the fall of the eighth wicket that West

---

[70]'Duleep Trophy Tournament', *Indian Cricket annual*, 1962, p. 254.

scrambled to a lead of 30 runs. But Central folded for a miserable 148 in their second innings and West won comfortably by eight wickets.

England were returning to tour India after the gap of a decade. The 1961–62 tour was only the second since Independence following the visit in 1951–52. India had marked the 1951–52 series by recording their first victory in Test cricket after 20 years and 25 Tests, winning the fifth and final at Madras' Corporation Stadium in February 1952. The series was drawn 1-1.

Unlike the Australians who always sent their best players, England till 1972–73 were content to send virtual second-string teams, with their leading players giving tours to both India and Pakistan a miss back then. Before the final squad was announced, a list of 29 probables was released. Eight of those stated they were unavailable including big names like Colin Cowdrey, Brian Close, Peter May, Fred Trueman and Brian Statham. The side was led by the dashing Ted Dexter and had in its ranks leading batsman Ken Barrington.

Leslie Smith commented in his tour summary in *Wisden Cricketers' Almanack* 1963, 'This business of leading players declining certain tours needs consideration by the authorities. India rightly point out that they have never seen a full-strength MCC [England] side and resent the fact that the star players make a habit of turning down the trip.'[71]

So Durani was back at the Brabourne Stadium, Bombay, for the first Test, the same venue where he had made his Test debut 11 months earlier. Once England batted well into the second day in piling up 500 for eight declared, the Test was

---

[71]Smith, Leslie, 'MCC Team in India, Pakistan and Sri Lanka, 1961–62', *Wisden Cricketers' Almanack 1963*, Norman Preston (ed.), Sporting Handbooks Ltd, London, 1963, p. 867.

destined for a draw. Durani's lone wicket in the first innings (he had two in the second) was the England captain bowled for 85 by an arm ball that went off his pads onto the stumps; it irked Dexter no end that he had been denied a century in his first Test on Indian soil and that too by a rookie. In just his second Test, Durani had the distinction of top scoring for India in the first innings. It was a knock full of dazzling strokes that had the crowd on its feet.

Fast bowler Alan Brown bounced, Durani narrowly evaded it. Next ball, another bouncer. This time it was hooked for six into the famous East Stand where he would have his biggest fan following over the years. There was also a lofted six off left-arm spinner Tony Lock.

It looked like nothing could stop him on his way to his maiden Test hundred. It took a sensational catch by Bob Barber at extra cover, who threw himself full length to catch the ball inches off the turf, to stop Durani's rampage. The bowler was off spinner David Allen. The innings of 71 contained 10 fours and two sixes. A new star had arrived on the stage of Indian cricket.

Raju Bharatan waxed eloquent, 'Durani launched that Sunday evening a terrific onslaught on the English bowlers, hooking, pulling, driving and cutting with refreshing abandon [...] Indeed his 71 was replete with some of the most sparkling strokes seen on a cricket ground.'[72]

Between the first Test at Bombay and the second at Kanpur there were three tour games. In the second of these, Durani became the first to score a century against the tourists with 124 for Rajasthan at Jaipur. It seemed he now had the measure of the English bowlers. The second and third Tests at Kanpur and Delhi were also drawn. At Kanpur, England were forced to

---

[72]Bharatan, Raju, 'Stars of Tomorrow: Salim Durani', *The Times of India*, 8 April 1962.

follow on by India for the first time in their history. At Delhi the last two days were washed out.

But there were dramatic developments off the field in Delhi that would rock Indian cricket and bring gloom to the camp.

Gupte's Injustice

The Imperial Hotel, located in the heart of downtown New Delhi, was inaugurated by Lord Willingdon in 1936. It still stands today in stately sparkling elegance amidst the dense traffic and thick pollution of the Capital.

During the Delhi Test, the players were staying at the hotel and with rain ruining the Test, they had plenty of time on their hands. Kripal Singh, single and in his 20s, took a fancy to the receptionist and called her for a date from Room No. 7, which he was sharing with Gupte. The young lady took exception and complained to the team manager. All hell broke loose.

Both players were summoned before the Board's disciplinary committee. Gupte was patently innocent—he was not even in the room when the call was made since he was playing cards with his teammates in another room at the time. Yet, both players were dropped for the next two Tests and also from the forthcoming tour of West Indies.

Gupte's sense of injustice was inflamed. Even Kripal exonerated him. In a fit of anger, Gupte lashed out at a board official and walked out not only from Test cricket but also from India altogether.

Gupte had met a young East Indian woman in Trinidad, Carol Goberdhan, on the first tour the Indians made to the West Indies in 1953. The tour was a striking success with the tourists drawing huge crowds. Up against the might of the legendary 'Three W's' of West Indies cricket, Frank Worrell, Clyde Walcott and Everton Weekes, the tourists lost just one of the five Tests with Gupte bowling brilliantly to capture 27 wickets. Garry Sobers, for one, has always maintained that Gupte was the best leg spinner he has ever seen, superior even to Australia's legendary Shane Warne.

But at the age of just 33, with at least five to six years of Test cricket still left in him and with a bag of 149 wickets in 36 Tests, Gupte was lost to Test cricket forever—all because his roommate had made an injudicious phone call. Gupte had married Carol in Bombay in 1957. They decided to settle permanently in San Fernando, Trinidad, where Carol's family was based. The scandalous manner in which the BCCI handled the issue was a slur on Indian cricket and Gupte carried the resentment till his passing in 2002.

In the memorable words of Mihir Bose, 'So India's first great spinner—if we classify Vinoo Mankad as an all-rounder—ended his career because he happened to share a room with a man who wanted a drink with a girl. Only in India could it have happened.'[73]

As for Kripal, he made a brief comeback to the Indian side in 1964. He died in Madras in 1987 but never spoke of the incident again.

Durani had only taken five wickets in the first three Test matches with Gupte, Kripal and Borde doing the bulk of the spin bowling. Despite that barnstorming 71 in the first Test, his place in the XI may have been in jeopardy for the fourth at Calcutta.

But now, with the exit of those two unfortunate souls, he had his foot in the door. Once again, destiny had played a part in his career just as it had when Jasu Patel's apparent illness allowed him to make his debut in January 1960. And once again the misfortune of others turned into good fortune for Destiny's Child.

---

[73]Bose, Mihir, *A History of Indian Cricket*, Andre Deutsch, London, 2002, p. 223.

Durani grabbed his chance with both hands—more accurately, his left. Even though there was gloom in the Indian camp after the Delhi incident, Contractor rallied his troops at Eden Gardens. In the enforced absence of Kripal and Gupte, the bowling onus was now on leg spinner Borde and Durani.

They both did well with the bat, too, as Borde (68) top scored and Durani hit a typically pugnacious 43 to help India to a healthy first innings total of 380. The biggest stumbling block for the Indian bowlers was Barrington, who had piled up runs with centuries in each of the three previous Tests.

For Salim, the Calcutta Test was memorable for another reason—he had a surprise meeting with his father! It was the first time they were meeting since Aziz walked out on the family in 1947 and moved to Pakistan. Master Aziz gave his son precious advice, and Durani produced a splendid delivery that bowled Barrington for 14 in the first innings. It was a similar ball that had accounted for Dexter in the first Test, the armer bowling Barrington off his pads. It was the crucial breakthrough, the first of his five wickets in the innings as England crashed to 212, handing India a big lead. Borde chipped in with four including the vital wicket of Dexter, who was bowled for 57.

This is how the Calcutta daily *The Statesman* described it after the fourth day's play, 'Durani had England's batsmen in sore perplexity with his left-arm spinners and it is a matter of some interest that he has had his inspiration from none other than Vinoo Mankad who has taken great interest in him and done much to bring him into the public eye. His bowling performance in the first innings will long be remembered.'[74]

India's second innings of 252 meant England's target was 421. Their only hope was to hold out for a draw after they lost four wickets by stumps on the fourth day. Durani accounted for

---

[74]'Our Cricket Correspondent', *The Statesman*, 5 January 1963.

the wicket of Bob Barber just before the close but it was his brilliant catch at backward short leg to send back Barrington off Desai's bowling that turned the tide India's way and raised visions of a rare victory. The previous nine Tests on Indian soil over the past 12 months had all ended in draws, so a result of this nature was sorely needed.

The biggest obstacle to victory for India was the English captain. But within 15 minutes on the final day he attempted a pull and was lbw to Durani for 62, his second half-century of the match. Now the floodgates were opened. Umrigar was leading in the absence of Contractor, who had injured his finger while fielding. He gave himself a long spell of 30 overs and was rewarded with the wickets of Peter Richardson and Peter Parffit. Fittingly, it was Durani who claimed the final wicket, last man David Smith caught by Manjrekar for two, and India had won the Test by the handsome margin of 187 runs.

Bowling figures of five for 47 and three for 66, plus 43 runs in the first innings and a brilliant catch—there were no Man of the Match awards back then but had there been, Durani would have been a shoo-in. Till date and after three decades of Test cricket, India had just two series victories to their credit. Would they now make it three?

Contractor deserves credit for not pulling down the shutters in the fifth and final Test at Madras. He would have been forgiven for deciding to sit on his lead and close out the series 1-0. But instead, he went for another win. It was Tiger Pataudi's bold attacking maiden Test century that set the tone on the opening day. Contractor's luck with the toss continued for the fourth time running. The captain/opener contributed 86 and with 60s from Nadkarni and Farokh Engineer, India crossed the 400-run mark for the third time in the series.

With off spinner E.A.S. Prasanna making his debut, the bowling was pretty spin-heavy. But Durani bowled the maximum overs in the Test, 36 in the first innings and 34 in the second innings. And he was richly rewarded for his toil. By close on the second day England had lost their top four batsmen, the biggest shock being the uncharacteristically cavalier batting of Barrington. He took one risk too many when he lofted Durani to mid-off and was splendidly caught by Manjrekar for 20.

From there it was an uphill task for the English. The third day belonged to Durani the bowler, as he took five of the six wickets that fell, finishing with six for 105, India's lead a substantial 147. With the pitch giving him assistance, the left-armer had all the batsmen groping helplessly, relying more on luck than skill.

Though the Indian batsmen—save for Manjrekar (85)—failed in the second innings, the total of 190 was more than enough. The target of 338 was always going to be too much of a mountain to climb for the English batsmen with the fifth-day pitch at Chepauk showing wear and tear. As it is, they had lost half their side by the end of the fourth day.

The varied bowling skills of Borde and Durani saw England all out for 209 and victory for India by 128 runs. It was the first time in seven series (two at home and five in England, including a one-off Test in 1932) that India had put it across to their old rulers and the wild celebrations that broke out across the country was understandable. It was in the same city of Madras 10 years earlier—though at a different stadium—that India had recorded its first win against England.

'CRICKET HISTORY MADE AT MADRAS; India win rubber against England; 128-RUN TRIUMPH IN FINAL TEST' was the bold banner headline in *The Statesman* dated 16 January 1962.

Durani's 10 wickets in the match saw him top both the averages and wickets tally not only for India but for both teams, with 23 wickets at 27.04. Added to this was his useful runs and smart catching. Surely a long and glittering career lay ahead of him. But in the words of John Lennon, 'Life is what happens to you while you're busy making other plans.'

As for Contractor, he was the toast of the nation for his innovative captaincy. No wonder a collage of his photos was featured on the cover of the *Sport & Pastime* annual for 1962. The annual also featured a colour poster of a beaming Durani that must have adorned the bedroom walls of young cricket fans around India.[75]

The series augured well for India with Engineer, Pataudi and Prasanna all making their debuts in this series and Durani cementing his place in the team.

Caribbean Crisis

The team left for the West Indies, if not exactly brimming with confidence about the formidable task ahead of them, then certainly with their morale high. Only two of the touring party, Manjrekar and Umrigar, had been part of the 1953 team, while there were nine first-time tourists in the 16-member touring party including Durani, Prasanna and vice captain Pataudi.

Little could they have imagined the disasters that would unfold over the next three months. It would go down in cricket history as the most traumatic tour of all, possibly only matched by England in the West Indies in 1981, when manager Ken Barrington died of a heart attack midway through a Test. There were two notable events back in India while the team was touring. First, Durani was informed he was the recipient of the Arjuna Award for sporting excellence instituted for the

---

[75] *Sport & Pastime* weekly was published by *The Hindu* group from 1947 to 1968. It was followed by *The Sportstar*, which was launched by the same group in 1978 and is still going strong.

first time by the government, making him the first cricketer to receive the honour.

Then in the Ranji Trophy it was once again Rajasthan versus Bombay in the final, as in 1960–61. But this time with Rajasthan missing Durani and Manjrekar on tour—to be fair, Bombay were without a number of their top players too—it was a total rout. Bombay, led by Madhav Apte, won by an innings and 287 runs on their home ground.

Up against one of the most formidable teams in the world, captained by the immortal Frank (later Sir Frank) Worrell, the Indians had little chance. They lost all five Tests and to add injury to insult, also lost their gallant captain for the last three Tests. He was struck a near-fatal blow on the head by the deadly Charlie Griffith in the tour match against Barbados, which was played between the second and third Tests. Griffith's suspect bowling action gave the whole episode a diabolical tone. In fact, he was no-balled for throwing by the square-leg umpire in the second innings.[76]

This shattered the morale and confidence of the Indians and the 21-year-old Nawab was now thrust into the hot seat of captaincy. As vice captain in only his second series, Pataudi was being groomed to take over from Contractor who, at 28, still had quite a few good years left in him. Sadly, he never played another Test match after the injury.

The might of the home team's batting—Worrell, Sobers, Rohan Kanhai, Conrad Hunte, et al., the thunderbolts of Wes Hall and the off spin of Lance Gibbs—proved too much for the hapless Indians. But there were sessions, even days, when they not only held their own, they even pushed back against the onslaught of their mighty opponents. This, despite missing

---

[76]Ezekiel, Gulu, *Myth-Busting: Indian Cricket Behind the Headlines*, Rupa Publications, New Delhi, 2021, p. 148–163.

their best bowler Subhash Gupte for non-cricket reasons and with a pace attack that proved ineffectual.

To top it all, the domestic season had started as early as August 1961, unheard-of really, and after five Tests against the English tourists, the Indians hardly had a break before embarking on this arduous tour. It was a punishing schedule which even full-time professional cricketers would have found too taxing. Rusi Surti, Umrigar and Durani were the standouts for India. Brunell Jones wrote in *Indian Cricket* annual 1962 in his tour summary, 'Durani's consistency showed him as an all-rounder of the highest stamp.'[77]

India were rocked on the opening day of the series at Port of Spain, Trinidad. They were in deep trouble at 89 for six, only for the two left-handed all-rounders, Durani (56) and Surti (57), to haul them past the 200-run mark.

Now it was the turn of Durani with the ball to bowl a mesmerizing spell. West Indies ended the second day struggling at 148 for six; three of those wickets falling to his probing line. 'Spin, "Magic, Mystical", Lures West Indies Stars to Their Doom'; 'A Great Day for India: Durani's Brilliant Role' were the dramatic headlines for K.N. Prabhu's report in *The Times of India*, 18 February 1962.

Hunte, Kanhai, Sobers and Worrell—the cream of the Caribbean batting was back in the pavilion. Borde and Umrigar gave Durani stellar support, accounting for the wickets of Kanhai and Sobers, respectively. Worrell found himself tied down by Durani. Famed for his attractive flair, the captain was marooned for 15 minutes without scoring. In desperation he even resorted to pad play. It was most uncharacteristic of him, and finally Durani put him out of his agony when he prodded

---

[77]Jones, Brunell, 'The Debacle in West Indies', *Indian Cricket annual*, 1962, p. 27.

forward, the ball deflecting off his pad for a simple catch to Surti at short leg, out for an inglorious duck. Umrigar had bowled Sobers for 40 at 136 for three; Worrell fell three runs later and just one run was added before Durani had opener Conrad Hunte caught and bowled for a painstaking 58. Three wickets had fallen for the addition of only four runs, and at 140 for five, the Indians were right back in the match. The packed crowd at the Queen's Park Oval—many of them were Indian supporters—were on their feet and when nightwatchman Charlie Stayers was caught by Borde off Durani, the total had limped to 148 for six at stumps.

Wrote Prabhu in *Sportsweek* annual 1970–71, 'In all the long years that I have watched Test cricket I have never sat through a more moving display of fighting cricket—of attacking bowling and livewire fielding—with not a run given away. With only a score of 203 before them, Kanhai and Sobers, Hunte and Nurse groped and fumbled against the spin of Durani and Borde. For all their subsequent tall scores, rarely did West Indies get the better of Durani. He was the master bowler of the series.'[78] *The Statesman's* report on the same date was headlined 'India's Spirited Fightback; Great Bowling by Durani'.[79]

The next day, the last four wickets nearly doubled the total and West Indies secured a lead of 86 runs. It was more than enough. The Indian batting crumbled in the second innings for a miserable 98 all out and West Indies romped home by 10 wickets. The Indians could only ruefully look back at their gallant display on the second day, the match ending a day early. West Indies recorded a crushing innings win in the second at Kingston, Jamaica.

---

[78]Prabhu, K.N., 'Memories of West Indies', *Sportsweek* annual *1970–71*.
[79]Bajnath, Hiralal, 'India's Spirited Fightback; Great Bowling by Durani', *The Statesman*, 18 February 1962.

With their captain still fighting for his life after multiple surgeries, the Indian camp led by the young Pataudi was in disarray when it moved to West Indies' fortress of Bridgetown, Barbados, for the third Test. This was the same ground where just days earlier Contractor had been struck by Griffith. They must have had their hearts in their mouths and it was no surprise really when they went down by an innings once again. Not one Indian batsman could reach 50 in the first innings of 258, with skipper Pataudi and Durani being joint top-scorers with 48. The home team's 475 was enough to win by an innings and 30 runs, to take an unbeatable 3–0 lead in the series.

It was back to Port of Spain for the fourth Test. The Queen's Park Oval has always been India's home-away-from-home in the Caribbean and here they put up their best performance of the entire series. This was almost entirely due to the magnificent displays by the veteran all-rounder Umrigar and Durani, the pretender to his throne.

The first innings followed the pattern of the series with West Indies piling up a big total (444) and the Indians crumbling (197). But the match took a dramatic turn when India followed on. Durani had batted at number nine in the first innings. But in the follow on he was promoted to one down with Sardesai running a fever. That changed the whole complexion of the innings. With opener M.L. Jaisimha falling cheaply, Vijay Mehra and Durani came together and took the attack to the bowlers. Their partnership was worth 144 runs at better than a run a minute. It was stirring stuff, especially since they had their backs to the wall in the match.

Mehra's 62 was the highest score of his eight-Test career, while Durani was at his flamboyant best. He repeatedly hooked Hall and Stayers, the short ball sent racing to the boundary. He reached his half-century in 78 minutes including nine boundaries, taking 14 runs off one Stayers' over. Mehra fell with the total at 163 and at stumps on the third day India were 186 for two, with Durani nine short of a maiden Test century and Manjrekar on nine.

In stark contrast to his batting the previous day, Durani was now overcome with nerves as he desperately tried to piece together the nine runs needed for his century even as wickets began to tumble at the other end, six falling in the first session itself. Durani was twice lucky as he advanced through the nineties, both off the bowling of Sobers who had him all at sea. At 96, he pushed a googly just short of Kanhai at backward short leg. On 99, Sobers tossed up a full toss and Durani almost fell for the bait, his hook dropped by Worrell at mid on. It was a nerve-wracking passage of play, but he finally got to his century, though he fell shortly after for 104. It would turn out to be the only century of his Test career. Now it was left to Umrigar. He took the bowling by the scruff of the neck and raced to 172 not out to go with his first innings 56 and five for 107 to match Mankad's grand all-round performance at Lord's in 1952.

India's highest total of the series (422) meant West Indies needed 176 to make it 4–0. It was never going to be a difficult task but they crawled to the winning total from 101 overs. Of these, Durani bowled 33 and he captured all three wickets to fall for 64 runs. Worrell became the first non-Australian captain to make a clean sweep of a five-Test series as India capitulated by 123 runs in the final Test at Kingston. Once again Durani was the leading Indian bowler with five wickets in the match.

Durani finished the series with the most wickets (17) for India. With one century and one 50, he lived up to his billing as the country's leading all-rounder. So impressed was Worrell that at the end of the series he clubbed Durani with the great Sobers as the world's leading all-rounders. While Sobers' batting and bowling figures for the series were far superior, Durani, it must be remembered, was up against vastly superior opposition.

Durani for his part picked Worrell as his all-time favourite cricketer, noting how graceful a batsman he was. They hit it off on the tour. Perhaps Worrell saw in him a kindred spirit, both on and off the field.

In fact, there had been a brief meeting between the two years earlier. While Worrell never toured India with the West Indian Test team, he did so three times with the Commonwealth XI who were popular tourists back then with players selected from around the cricket world. On his second visit, the team played a match against Saurashtra at Rajkot in October 1950. The cricket-mad schoolboy Salim made the 90-km journey by train from Jamnagar every morning and so entranced was he by Worrell's style and elegance that he managed to wangle an introduction to his new idol by Vinoo Mankad. Twelve years later they would be face-to-face in a Test series.

One teammate of his on the tour who was hugely impressed was the young Prasanna. 'On [this] tour I looked upon Salim as some sort of God. He had the measure of the powerful West Indies batting machine with the masterly effort of controlled spin. I saw the great Sobers, the immaculate Worrell and the tempestuous Kanhai shackled by him. That he didn't get a larger number of wickets, as he should have, was sheer bad luck [...] He faced the fire of West Indies pace with exemplary courage [...] Salim was a hooker, rare and brave.'[80]

Berry Sarbadhikary, one of the most widely travelled Indian cricket journalists of his time, had this to say about Durani's skills, 'Durani's competence as a left-arm spinner of quality is perhaps best reflected in the fact that out of his 25 wickets on the Caribbean tour, 17 were obtained in the Tests. And this was in the wake of his 23 wickets at home against England in 1961–62. With the bat he can be brilliant [...] this marks him out

---

[80]Prasanna, E.A.S., *One More Over*, Rupa Publications, New Delhi, 1978, p. 85.

The pavilion at the Jamnagar cricket ground where Durani learnt the basics of the game.
Photo by Aditya Bhushan

The young Salim towering over his Bombay Schools teammates in 1951–52.
Photo courtesy: Theo Braganza, The Marine Sports

Statue of Vinoo Mankad in Jamnagar. Coach, mentor and teammate of Durani.

Photo by Aditya Bhushan

The ground at Commerce College (now HL Commerce College) in Navrangpura, Ahmedabad, where Durani scored a century on Ranji Trophy and first-class debut in November 1953.

Photo by Anita Agarwal

The Rajasthan team which entered the final of the Ranji Trophy for the first time in 1960-61. Durani is standing in the centre. To his left is Rusi Surti. Hanumnat Singh is sitting extreme left while Raj Singh Dungarpur seated in the centre.

Photo courtesy: Rameshwar Singh

The Queen's Park Oval in Port of Spain, Trinidad. The scene of Durani's greatest Test match feats in 1962 and 1971.

Photo by Ian Subhash Mohan

The pavilion at the Great Chell cricket ground in England where Durani played for one season in 1963.

Photo courtesy: The Sentinel, Stoke-on-Trent

The Indian team in the West Indies in 1971. Captain Ajit Wadekar is sitting fourth from left. To his right is Durani. Sunil Gavaskar is standing extreme left.

Photo courtesy: Craig Cozier

Durani (Cenral Zone) gets the vital wicket of opener Sunil Gavaskar (West Zone), caught by Suryaveer Singh for 30 in the first innings of the Duleep Trophy final at Bangalore in March 1972.

Photo by Hosey Mistry

The victorious Central Zone team that won the Duleep Trophy for the first time, beating West Zone in the final in March 1972. Captain Hanumant Singh is standing fourth from left with Durani standing extreme left.

Photo by Hosey Mistry

Durani walks out to bat in the Ranji Centenary match at Jamnagar in September 1972.
Photo courtesy: Rameshwar Singh

Durani pulls England off spinner Pat Pocock for six in the 5th and final Test at Brabourne Stadium in February 1973.

Photo by Gopal Bhat; courtesy: Raj Bhat

Walking out to bat with G.R. Vishwanath in the fifth Test at Bombay, the final Test of his career.

Photo by Gopal Bhat; courtesy: Raj Bhat

His last bow: Durani's final Test innings comes to an end as he is caught by England wicket-keeper Alan Knott off Pat Pocock for 37 in the Bombay Test.

Photo by Hosey Mistry

The Indian team lines up at the end of the series against England at the Brabourne Stadium, Bombay in February 1973. Captain Ajit Wadekar is fifth from right with Tiger Patuadi to his left. Durani is third from left.

Photo by Gopal Bhat; courtesy: Raj Bhat

On location at Poona with Parveen Babi for the shooting of the movie *Charitra* in 1973.

Publicity still

Durani with the legendary quartet of spinners. From the left: S. Venkataraghavan, Bishan Singh Bedi, Durani, E.A.S. Prasanna, B.S. Chandrasekhar.

Photo courtesy: Boria Majumdar; The Illustrated History of Indian Cricket.

Durani with India teammate Farokh Engineer.

Photo courtesy: Rameshwar Singh

Durani with Rajasthan and Central Zone teammate Parthasarthi Sharma.
Photo courtesy: Rameshwar Singh

Pictured at his home in Jamnagar in 2017 with the C.K. Nayudu Lifetime Achievement Award presented to him by the BCCI in 2011.

Photo by *Aditya Bhushan*

Durani with Sunil Gavaskar on the opening day of the inaugural India–Afghanistan Test match at Bengaluru on 14 June 2018.

Amul's moving tribute to Durani after his passing.
Courtesy: Amul & DaCunha Communications

as an all-rounder of great merit. He can be, however, somewhat moody and needs nursing and careful handling.'[81] It meant that Durani had now taken 40 wickets in his last 10 Tests. But that tag of 'moody' was already thrust upon him so early in his career and something he could never shake off. Even his great friend and fan Prasanna described him as 'moody and sensitive', adding that 'these are the traits of a genius.'[82]

Continuing on the genius theme, cricket journalist Suresh Menon wrote after Durani's passing, 'The great off spinner Erapalli Prasanna once sent me a picture of the Fabulous Four—Bishan Bedi, Bhagwat Chandrasekhar, Venkataraghavan and himself—with a note saying "Genius in the middle." The genius was Salim Durani.'[83]

Career Choices

After the West Indies tour, Durani received an offer to join the Spencer's company in Madras, which ran one of the most high-profile departmental stores in the country, and he shifted there in late 1962. The offer was extended to him by one of the company directors, Zal Irani, a treasurer and president of the BCCI after whom the Irani Cup (launched in 1959–60) was named. Durani also represented Jolly Rovers club in the 1962–63 season in the highly competitive Madras Cricket Association first division league. The club was then run and led by S. Rangarajan of *The Hindu* media group before being taken over by India Cements. Durani's salary was ₹2,000 per month (plus boarding and lodging expenses) which today would be the equivalent of

---

[81]Sarbadhikary, Berry, *My World of Cricket: A Century of Tests*, Cricket Library, Calcutta, 1964, p. 101.
[82]Prasanna, E.A.S., *One More Over*, Rupa Publications, New Delhi, 1978, p. 83.
[83]Menon, Suresh, 'Salim Durani and the Vulnerabilities of Genius', *The Hindu*, 6 April 2023, http://tinyurl.com/bdfju29b. Accessed on 15 February 2024.

₹1.65 lakh. Back then, Indian cricketers were paid ₹50 for each day a Test match and if the match ended early the daily allowance—referred to as 'smoke money'—would be deducted.

Spencer's was the first fancy departmental store in the country and the first to have an escalator in the 1930s. It had the best of Indian goods plus some British items and was frequented by the wealthy of Madras.

Durani had hoped to represent Madras in the Ranji Trophy that season. But he did not fulfil the residential qualifications under the tournament rules (22B) which stated, 'A cricketer shall be eligible to play for the association within the limits of whose jurisdiction he has resided bona fide from November 1 of the year prior to the tournament.' Since he was not able to get leave from the company either, he was also not able to represent Rajasthan. And no foreign team visited that season for a Test series.

Thus he missed an entire season of first-class cricket save for two minor tournaments in which he made little impact in three games. This was one in the Moin-ud-Dowlah Gold Cup invitational tournament in Hyderabad in October 1962, followed by two in the National Defence Fund series. Sans their new star, Rajasthan made it to the Ranji Trophy final for the third time running and for the third time they were beaten by Bombay. It meant that Durani had missed the last two finals. The arrangement with Spencer's in Madras did not last long and by the next year he was back representing Rajasthan.

Before the Madras sojourn, he had a job with a pharmaceutical firm in Bombay where he also played in the numerous tournaments in the city. He met his first wife Rekha, a dancer in South Indian movies, and they had a daughter. The marriage did not last, though.

Durani was back for Rajasthan for the 1963–64 season. And for the fourth season running it was Rajasthan versus Bombay in the final, with the predictable result: victory for Bombay yet again. For Rajasthan's star it was a triumphant return and he turned in a fabulous all-round performance. He was the second highest run getter for the state and captured the second-most wickets as well.

In their opening match against Madhya Pradesh, he showed a different side to his batting. Rajasthan were struggling at 80 for four after Madhya Pradesh were all out for 170. Durani buckled down, eschewing his usual flamboyance and reached his 100 with only 13 boundaries, unusual in his case. Rajasthan won by nine wickets.

It was as a bowler that he excelled next, against Vidarbha with five wickets for 26 as they collapsed for 132 and Rajasthan took the honours. They sealed the top spot in the league when they beat Uttar Pradesh by five wickets in the third and final zonal match. Durani had five wickets in the match and scored 37 in the first innings.

The semi-final against Delhi was at Jaipur's Railway Ground. Here it was the Nawab of Pataudi captaining Delhi against Rajasthan's Raj Singh of Dungarpur. The visiting batsmen floundered on the unfamiliar coir matting with Rajasthan's pace trio of G.R. Sunderam, Raj Singh and Kailash Gattani taking all but two wickets, which were claimed by Durani. Delhi's miserable total of 126 was easily overcome by Rajasthan, who gained a lead of 105 runs. Durani thrilled the cheering home crowd as he raced to 37 in 36 minutes, twice hooking bouncers from Test pace bowler Rajinder Pal for sixes.

Delhi did much better in the second innings. Future Test batsman Ramesh Saxena played a brilliant innings of 151 and Delhi with 330 set Rajasthan 226 to win. The prized wicket of Pataudi fell to Durani. The Delhi skipper was batting confidently and had reached 21 when the bowler lured him into a lofted drive which landed in the hands of Suryaveer Singh at extra cover. This was the second of his three wickets in the innings and, once again, he had played his part as Rajasthan were home by five wickets.

Grand Century

So, for the fourth season running, it was Bombay versus Rajasthan for the title. Predictably, Bombay emerged winners by nine wickets. This time, though, it was not as easy as it looked. Raj Singh surprised one and all by asking the champions to bat after winning the toss. On the Brabourne Stadium pitch there could be only one result of such a move—a massive Bombay total of 526.

Rajasthan's batting was in shambles. From 21 for five they crumbled to 108, conceding a massive lead and having to follow on. Only Durani showed some resistance with 30 fighting runs, stretched out over 150 minutes. Having missed the two previous finals against Bombay, here was Durani's chance to show how much Rajasthan needed him. The three stars of Rajasthan—Durani, Manjrekar and Hanumant—all scored centuries as Rajasthan piled up 438. It was a grand, though futile, fightback.

The expert opinion was that Durani outshone his more illustrious teammates with his glorious knock of 118. Coming up against the giants of domestic cricket, it was an innings he was rightly proud of his entire life, just as he was of his eight wickets against the same giants in the 1960–61 final. Wrote Dicky Rutnagur in his match report in *The Indian Cricket Field Annual 1964–65*, 'He was in full cry and one had no second thoughts about the Brabourne Stadium being his favourite ground. When in form Durani can hardly be surpassed for either elegance or the punitive power of his strokes.'[84] He dominated the third wicket partnership of 157 runs with Manjrekar, an international batsman of impeccable credentials.

Rusi Modi was equally effusive in *Indian Cricket* annual 1964, 'The innings that appealed to me the most [of the three centuries] was that of the lanky Durani. The crowd held breathlessly on each stroke as he pulled and drove past cover with effortless ease [...] he is an artist of variable moods.'[85]

England Again

There was a gap of 10 years between the visits of the first post-Independence English team to tour India in 1951–52 and the next in 1961–62. But now the English were back after just two years, this time led by M.J.K. (Mike) Smith. It was also the first full series in which Pataudi captained India.

The five Tests all ended in draws. This was the third time the Indian team had been involved in such a dire result since 1954–55 and the second time in India. Fortunately, it has never happened again in the history of Test cricket; although when England toured India in 1981–82 for six Tests, India won the first and the next five were drawn.

The tourists in fact did well to avoid the defeat suffered at the hands of Dexter's men on the earlier tour, considering the number of players who were either injured or fell ill. At times, they struggled to put 11 men on the field and had to fly in emergency replacements.

With no team visiting India the previous season (1962–63), the Indian crowds were looking forward to some exciting

---

[84]Dicky Rutnagur, 'Cricket Championship of India for the Ranji Trophy 1963–64', *The Indian Cricket Field Annual 1964–65*, p. 307.
[85]Modi, Rusi, 'Ranji Trophy Matches', *Indian Cricket annual*, 1964, p. 195.

cricket. That was not to be. A combination of placid pitches and below-par bowling meant it was the batsmen who dominated. Neither captain was willing to take too much of a risk in going for a result either.

Durani, who had been the star bowler with 23 wickets in the previous home series, only managed to bag 11 this time around. Between him and Borde, they had claimed 39 wickets against Dexter's men. This time, they could only manage 20. Durani's bowling lacked the bite he had shown both at home and in the Caribbean. The other left-arm spinner Nadkarni created a world record of sorts. In the first innings of the first Test at Madras, he had the remarkable figures of 32-27-5-0 including a run of 21.5 maidens (131 balls) without conceding a single run, as England crawled to 317 from 190.4 overs.

Once again it was his favourite Brabourne Stadium that brought out the best in Durani in the second Test. Coming in at 99 for six in the first innings, he and his comrade-in-arms Borde salvaged the batting with a partnership worth 153 runs. Durani's batting was a mix of regal and streaky shots. Unlike when he was approaching his century at Port of Spain in 1962, this time he made a number of risky strokes as he came close to what would have been the second hundred of his Test career. With his score on 90, he glanced debutant fast bowler John Price and was caught down the leg side by fellow-debutant wicketkeeper Jimmy Binks. He had batted for 183 minutes and hit 11 boundaries. A notable debutant on the Indian side was Mysore leg spinner B.S. Chandrasekhar, who would have a long and illustrious career ahead of him as one of India's greatest match-winning bowlers.

Durani had his best bowling figures of the series (three for 59) in England's first innings, including a fantastic catch off his own bowling as he went sprawling forward to grasp the tentative push from left-hander Don Wilson. India escaped with a draw in the fifth and final Test at Kanpur. Replying to England's huge 559 for eight declared, they had to follow on after replying with 266. The Test and series was saved with India then piling up 347 for three. Nadkarni's unbeaten 122 was his maiden Test century and, like his fellow left-hander, it would be his lone one too.

As for Durani, he took advantage of England, employing their non-regular bowlers as the match petered out into another draw, smashing 61 not out with five boundaries and three sixes. He raced to 50 from 36 balls in 29 minutes, just a minute slower than the prevalent world record and still a record for an Indian. But overall, it was a disappointing series for India's best all-rounder, finishing low down in both the batting and bowling averages.

A Packed Season

The 1964–65 season was the busiest yet for Indian cricket. For the first time, the twin-tour system was carried out with Australia playing three Tests and New Zealand following with four. In between, Ceylon (now Sri Lanka) also visited for three unofficial Tests.

Durani was here, there and everywhere, playing against all the international sides as well as in the Ranji and Duleep Trophy and the Irani and Moin-ud-Dowlah Gold Cup.

The biggest shock in the Ranji Trophy were Rajasthan—finalists the last three seasons—being edged out by Uttar Pradesh for the top spot in the zone, thus failing to qualify for the knockout for the first time since the tournament pattern was changed to the league-cum-knockout system in 1957–58.

The other big surprise, and a very pleasant one at that for Indian followers, was the shocking defeat of Australia in the second Test at Bombay. Bob Simpson had led Australia to victory in the Ashes series in England just months earlier, just as Benaud had beaten England in Australia before tasting defeat at Kanpur in the 1959–60 series. So on both occasions the Australian tourists were holders of the Ashes.

The series ended deadlocked at 1–1 following Australia's win in the first Test at Madras and a draw in the third and final at Calcutta. Indian cricket thus had much to celebrate, especially since the Aussies, unlike the English, always sent their top players to India. A team containing Simpson, Bill Lawry, Norman O'Neill, Peter Burge, Ian Redpath, Neil Hawke and Graham McKenzie was world-class. So the thrilling victory by two wickets at Bombay was certainly sweet and made even sweeter when India won the series that followed against the Kiwis 1–0.

Durani had a quiet time in the first two Tests though he had an engrossing battle with the formidable O'Neill at Madras before he bowled him for 40. But at Bombay he was totally ineffective. He was on the verge of losing his place in the side before coming into his own at Calcutta, where rain washed out almost half the match. P.N. Sundaresan in *Indian Cricket* annual 1965 wrote, 'He was a man of moods and seemed to need a lot of coaxing to get into his best form.'[86]

Once again, the 'M' word had been used to describe his temperament. It was even there in the caption to a photo which was published during the series. Was this just a lazy cliché, a convenient tag? Surely there must have been more than a grain of truth to it if so many teammates and journalists kept repeating it just a few years into his international career? And now Nadkarni was stealing a march over his more flamboyant—and 'moody'—teammate as he was the top wicket-taker for India with 17. In the competition for the left-arm spinner's slot, Durani was falling behind.

---

[86]Sundaresan, P.N., 'Challenge Accepted', *Indian Cricket annual 1965*, p. 1.

The spell in Calcutta was spectacular though. Simpson and Lawry had added 97 for the opening wicket without any trouble when Durani struck, bowling the left-handed Lawry for 50. In one over he had three wickets including two from successive deliveries as Australia slumped to 109 for four. Bob Cowper was caught by Nadkarni for four at 104 for two, and then Burge and Brian Booth fell in successive balls. Redpath was surrounded by fielders for the hat-trick delivery but survived and clung on for 32 not out as the Australian batting folded for 174. Durani's 28-11-73-6 would be the best bowling analysis of his Test career. His place was now secure, at least in the short term.

The domestic season continued between the two series with the disappointment surrounding Rajasthan being offset to some extent with Central Zone reaching the Duleep Trophy final for the first time. Once again, Durani showed his batting skills at his favourite Brabourne. Though he was a flop with the ball and West won by an innings, it was Durani who stood out with scores of 42 and a delightful 119 against a quality bowling attack of Desai, Surti, Nadkarni and Baloo Gupte.

The first three Tests against New Zealand at Madras, Calcutta and Bombay were all drawn though they were exciting moments, particularly at Bombay. India were forced to follow on but came charging back to such an extent that the visitors were hanging on for a draw by the end. The fourth and final in Delhi ended in victory for India by seven wickets. Here, too, there was plenty of excitement towards the close with India needing 70 to clinch the Test and series in the 70 minutes remaining on the final day. They reached the target in 9.1 overs. The outstanding performance came from the teenage Madras off spinner S. Venkataraghavan who had made his debut in the first Test. With eight wickets in the first innings and four in the second, he troubled all the Kiwi batsmen and finished with 21 wickets in the series.

Durani was dropped for this Test. It was the first time since the first Test against England back in November 1960 that he found himself out of the playing XI, a run of 21 Tests in which he claimed 71 wickets. In the three Tests of the series he had nine wickets and finished second in the averages, next only to Venkat, the teenage sensation. Nadkarni, his competitor for the slot, was way down with just four wickets in four Tests. It appears his batting form was held against Durani, a highest of only 34 in five innings. But then Nadkarni did not do much better either.

With Nadkarni flopping, Chandra and Venkat had to be given extensive bowling stints in the first innings. Chandra bowled 37 overs and Venkat 51.1, while in the second it was 34 and 61.2, respectively. Together they captured 16 of the 19 wickets that fell to the bowlers (one run out). Nadkarni bowled 35 overs in the match without taking a single wicket.

Wrote P.N. Sundaresan in *Sport & Pastime*, 'The gap between the quality of these two spinners and the rest was so much that Pataudi was hard put to maintain the hostility of the attack [...] He really missed Durani, whose penetration on a responsive wicket was proved both at Bombay and Calcutta, very much. And in his absence he overworked them so much that Venkataraghavan lost some of his bite in the closing stages while Chandrasekhar had to retire with pain in the hip.'[87]

So, on the face of it, the decision to drop Durani was unjust. But it was only a taste of what was to come.

---

[87]Sundaresan, P.N., 'Time to Tourists' Rescue', *Sport & Pastime*, 3 April 1965.

Four

Exile and Trauma (1965–66 to 1969–70)

Before the Internet, before even computers, cricket lovers and journalists alike would hunt down books and magazines—a task that was all the more challenging in India—that contained profiles of players. One of the most popular reference books of this kind, *World Cricketers: A Biographical Dictionary*, the richest and most comprehensive encyclopaedia of its kind, was written by the late journalist and broadcaster Christopher Martin-Jenkins. It was so popular that it was released in three updated editions over the years with profiles of cricketers, Test and non-Test, as well as journalists, administrators and others connected with the game.

The third and final edition released in 1996 had 250 entries in the India section, and this is an extract of the Durani profile, 'An erratically brilliant left-handed batsman who could hit courageously or defend dourly, Durani was a slow-arm bowler who, despite a rather lazy looking action, could attract nip from the pitch and subtly vary changes of flight and line. Always aggressive, he often produced balls that beat batsmen at the top of their form.' He also refers to Durani as 'tall and handsome'.[88]

---

[88]Martin-Jenkins, Christopher, *World Cricketers: A Biographical Dictionary*, Oxford University Press, New York, 1996, p. 426.

Having been dropped for the first time since making his Test debut in January 1960, Durani's focus was now on getting back into the national side, and so he had to prove himself once again on the domestic circuit. After missing out on making it five finals in a row in the 1964–65 season, Rajasthan once again met their old nemesis Bombay in the final in 1965–66—the fifth time in six seasons—with the predictable result. But Rajasthan only made it to the final by the skin of their teeth. Having swept past Services in the quarter-final, they came up against a rampant Mysore in the semi-final at Bangalore. Their young spinners E.A.S. Prasanna and B.S. Chandrasekhar were in top form and came within a wicket of making it to the final.

In reply to Mysore's 397, Rajasthan led comfortably on the first innings after piling up 458. Vijay Manjrekar's splendid 175 was the highlight. Mysore declared their second innings at 243 for seven and threw down a challenge to their gallant opponents—get 183 in 180 minutes or sit on your lead and make it to the final. To their great credit, Rajasthan picked up the gauntlet. But in going for an outright victory, they almost came to grief. Rajasthan's wickets began to tumble and, with 50 minutes remaining, they needed 45 runs with just three wickets standing.

The ninth wicket fell at 166. It took a nerve-wracking last wicket stand between Raj Singh Dungarpur (20) and last man G.R. Sunderam (12) to see them home, with the Bangalore crowd and all the players on tenterhooks. Prasanna was the tragic hero with seven of the nine wickets to fall and five in the first.

After that scare, the final on coir matting at Jaipur's Railway Cricket Ground came as an anticlimax. It was a no-contest as Bombay ran out winners by eight wickets for their eighth straight title win. The match was over as a contest before tea on the first day itself, as the hosts crumbled to 125 all out.

Even before the start, they received a major jolt when their leading batsman, Manjrekar, pulled out with a sudden attack of appendicitis. Future national captain Ajit Wadekar was the star of the season and his 185 shut out Rajasthan. Durani once again failed with bat and ball, and despite a century in the league stage against Madhya Pradesh, it was a disappointing season for him.

One memory stood out though, for Amrit Mathur. A well-known sports administrator who became a close friend of Durani, he was witnessing the match as a child. Durani's 29 was the top score in the miserable first innings. 'My lasting memory is Salim Bhai hitting Ramakant Desai for six—the ball sailed over square leg to land on the railway track, a monster hit. After the game, I stood in a queue to get my autograph book signed by him.'[89] In fact, it landed a good 120 yards—a monster hit indeed. 'Tiny' Desai was quite the terror back then, the fastest bowler in India whose bouncer troubled even the original Little Master, Pakistan's Hanif Mohammad.

There was some consolation with Central Zone reaching the Duleep Trophy final for the second season in succession, once again finishing on the losing side. With Chandrasekhar and Prasanna in devastating form, Central were bowled out for 123 and 167 to lose by an innings and 20 runs to South. Durani top scored in both innings with 36 and 40 and also captured five wickets in South's total of 310.

The season had kicked off with the Irani Cup and Durani was representing Rest of India for the first time in this, the fourth edition of the match against the Ranji Trophy champions. This fixture had been launched in 1959–60. With more than half the match being washed out in Madras, Rest and Bombay

---

[89]Mathur, Amrit, 'Chater 5: Salim Durani', *My Cricket Hero: XII Indians on Their XII Favourite Cricketers*, Gulu Ezekiel (ed.), Rupa Publications, New Delhi, 2022, p. 37.

were declared joint winners as the first innings could not be completed. Durani coming low down in the order at number 10 was 49 not out.

West Indian Visitors

West Indies had been slated to tour India for the third time in 1965–66. But a delay in the release of precious foreign exchange by the government to the BCCI saw the series pushed to 1966–67. Again, there was a question mark over it as £18,000 was being held back considering the acute financial crisis the country was facing. Finally it happened at the personal intervention of Prime Minister Indira Gandhi, who had just recently assumed office. However, as a compromise, the Board had to agree to a truncated series of only three Tests instead of the usual five. How times have changed!

Just as Australia under Richie Benaud in 1959–60 and then under Bob Simpson in 1964–65 were unofficial world champions when they visited India, so, this West Indian side was considered the best in the world. They were coming to India hot on the heels of a comprehensive 3–1 series win in England earlier in the year, and had a formidable batting and bowling unit with captain Garry Sobers now universally recognized as the best batsman and leading all-rounder in world cricket. Worrell had handed the reins to his heir apparent and protégé who, in his first series as leader, had defeated Australia 2–1 at home in 1965. But Sobers and his men did not quite dominate. The 2–0 scoreline in their favour was somewhat misleading. India could have saved the first Test at Bombay which they lost and could have won the third at Madras which was drawn. The second at Calcutta deserves a chapter of its own.

Durani was back at the Brabourne where he had made his Test debut in January 1960. Of course he would have had no inkling that this would be his last Test match for nearly four-and-a-half years. Two left-handed batsmen, Ajit Wadekar and Clive Lloyd, were making their Test debuts and would go onto captain their teams in the years to come.

India chose to bat on winning the toss but were jolted by the loss of three wickets with only 14 runs on the board. Chandu Borde was holding the fort with his fourth and penultimate Test century. He would score his final century in the third Test at Madras. The first recovery act was with his captain Pataudi, adding 93 for the fourth wicket. Subsequently, with his buddy Durani, a century stand for the sixth wicket hauled India to a respectable 296.

Durani's was a sparkling innings of 55 studded with nine boundaries and a six. In one over from the fearsome Charlie Griffith, he smashed 15 runs including a hooked six off a bouncer. He was dropped on 11 by David Holford off his cousin Sobers' bowling. The partnership was terminated at 240 for six when he was bowled by Sobers attempting a rash shot head in the air just minutes before stumps on the opening day. But then that was how he played his cricket—a mix of flamboyance and carelessness.

The visitors also overcame early setbacks with Chandra having them in all sorts of trouble, taking the first three wickets with 82 on the board. Opener Conrad Hunte was standing firm with 101 before Durani bowled him for his only wicket in the match. The middle order all contributed and West Indies chalked up a lead of 125. Chandra had figures of seven for 157 in a superb display of leg spin bowling. He would prove to be West Indies's nemesis over the next decade.

India's lower order came good in the second innings and West Indies were set a target of 192. They got there but not before Chandra captured their first four wickets with 90 on the board. Lloyd and Sobers took them home by six wickets. But it was Chandra who turned in the outstanding performance of the Test with 11 of the 15 West Indian wickets to fall while bowling one third of India's overs.

Former Test batsman Rusi Modi was critical of Durani's bowling in his match report for *Playfair Cricket Monthly*, 'Instead of flighting the ball, he pushed it through much faster than expected of a bowler of his "genre". As a result, he made no impression on the batsmen [...] and did not bowl to his field.'[90]

Calcutta Shocker

While Durani's bowling had been ineffectual—43 overs for just one wicket—his batting (55 and 17) should have been enough for him to retain his place for the second Test at Eden Gardens. A shocking series of events, however, saw him out for Calcutta as well as Madras. To add to that, he was also dropped for the tours of England, Australia and New Zealand that followed in 1967–68.

So what was the story behind his dropping? Over the years, Durani has narrated how he could arrive in Calcutta only the night before the first day of the Test as his wife was seriously ill and had been hospitalized in Bombay. The manager, Col Hemu Adhikari, a strict disciplinarian who tended to treat cricketers like kids, was furious and told him to return. However, there is a twist to the tale, one that Durani narrated to Rameshwar Singh—a piece of information that has never been revealed in print before. (It should be noted here that Rameshwar was a close confidant of Durani.)

Even as he was sitting in the lobby of the Calcutta hotel ruminating on his fate, in walked Manindranath Dutta Ray, aka

---

[90]Modi, Rusi, 'West Indies Win Despite Chandrasekhar', *Playfair Cricket Monthly*, February 1967.

Bechu Babu, the chairman of the selectors. Durani opened a newspaper and pretended to read as he did not want to face him. Thinking that Dutta Ray had passed him, Durani stretched out his long legs and promptly tripped the former and sent him sprawling across the lobby floor! And to make matters worse, other BCCI officials who came trooping in after him were also witness to the sorry spectacle. A livid Dutta Ray accused Durani of deliberately tripping him out of malice, a charge that he vehemently denied.[91]

Was that the reason he was shunned all those years? One can never know for sure. Vijay Merchant took over as chairman in September 1968 with Dutta Ray back as the East Zone representative. But when in January 1971 the team to tour West Indies was chosen, Dutta Ray was not present at the meeting under most unusual circumstances.

A report in *Sportsweek* looking back at his dropping expressed surprise, 'Durani, a graceful lefthander was considered to be the most useful all-rounder in Indian cricket in the 60s. In recent years, he had fallen off considerably in the esteem of the selectors. He had very few backers. A veteran of 23 Tests, Durani played his last Test against West Indies [in 1966]. He had scored a fine 55 in the Bombay Test and was in the list of 16 probables for the Calcutta Test. He was not chosen in the final eleven and was not even considered to fill up the eleventh hour vacancy created by Ajit Wadekar's indisposition.'[92]

(The report appeared after the December 1970 Irani Cup match in which Durani scored a century and shortly before the team to West Indies was announced. These events will be taken up in greater detail in Chapter Five.)

So, who was Dutta Ray, the representative from the East

---

[91] Conversation between Rameshwar Singh and author on 8 July 2023.
[92] 'Durani, Jaisimha Back In Form', *Sportsweek*, 3 January 1971.

Zone? He remains the only selector never to have played first-class cricket though he was an umpire in the early years of the Ranji Trophy. Remarkably, he had a run of 20 years on the national selection committee from 1951–52 to 1971–72, including as chairman from 1963–64 to 1966–67. In those years, he wielded tremendous clout not only in cricket but also in football as chairman of the selection committee of the All India Football Federation, an unprecedented 'double' so to speak in Indian sporting history. To add to that, he was also a founder member of the Indian Olympic Association.

Dutta Ray's pride and joy was his Sporting Union club, which currently competes in the Cricket Association of Bengal (CAB) first division league while its football team languishes in the fourth division of the Calcutta league. His diktat was simple—play for my cricket club if you harbor ambitions of being selected for the Indian team. Two casualties of his ego and malice in the 1960s were batsman Shyam Sundar Mitra and pace bowler Samir Chakrabarti, both with brilliant first-class records that surely should have seen them gain national honours. But both turned down his offer to play for his beloved club and thus paid a heavy price.

But one man's misfortune turned out to be another's stroke of luck. Durani's absence from the second Test—and that of the other left-arm spinner, Nadkarni, who was also dropped—saw the debut of young Punjab left-arm spinner Bishan Singh Bedi—a bowler (and future captain) who would adorn the game for the next decade with his guile, skill, passion and fighting spirit. He had just celebrated his twentieth birthday and was the last of the famed quartet to make his debut. The other three, Prasanna, Chandrasekhar and Venkataraghavan, had already made their mark.

Bedi had played two matches against the tourists. In the opening match of the tour for Combined Universities at Hyderabad, he failed to take a wicket but still impressed. Then, between the Bombay and Calcutta Tests playing for Prime Minister's XI at New Delhi, he returned excellent figures of 51-11-129-6 including the wickets of Lloyd and Sobers. This match incidentally was the first in India to be telecast live on *Doordarshan*, though the signal was only available within the Lutyens' Delhi area and on the handful of sets in the Capital at the time.

On the eve of the Test, Bedi was getting ready to leave for Chandigarh for the Inter-Varsity tournament when someone told him he had heard on the radio that he had been selected in the XI. He had not been told formally of his selection but, when he met Pataudi in his room, the captain confirmed the news. Bedi too has written about his mysterious entry into the playing XI. 'When I was asked to report in Calcutta [before the Test] I was not actually part of the squad. I flew there carrying my hold-all, just in case I had to return by train for my university engagements. India had Durani and Nadkarni in the team and I had no hope of playing. I might have bowled reasonably well in the nets, for it helped me get the nod from Mansur Ali Khan Pataudi.'[93]

The Contrasts

It was the first time in 24 Tests over six years that neither Durani nor Nadkarni would be in the playing XI. Together they had played in 19 Tests including Durani's debut in January 1960 against Australia at Bombay.

Durani would not play another Test till early 1971. In the 1960s (1960 to 1966), in which he played in those 24 Tests, he

---

[93]Bedi, Bishan Singh, 'Establishing the Indian Identity', *India 500 Tests: The Journey Began in 1932*, Ayon Sengupta (ed.), Kasturi & Sons Ltd, Chennai, 2016, p. 24.

captured 71 wickets. This was the third most in the decade for India after Prasanna's 113 (who made his debut in January 1962) in 22 Tests and Nadkarni (who made his debut in December 1955) with 76 in 33 Tests. Nadkarni had a total of 88 from 41 Tests at the Strike Rate (SR) of a wicket every 104.1 balls, while Durani's SR was 85.9.

I once asked Bedi for his opinion of Nadkarni's bowling. He paused for a moment, drew a sharp intake of breath, and muttered that it was 'too defensive'. His seeming disdain was not surprising since Bedi's own philosophy in life as well as in cricket had always been attack–attack–attack. Nadkarni's defensiveness is reflected in his amazing economy rate (ER). For those bowlers with 75 or more Test wickets, Nadkarni with 1.67 runs per over is second only to South Africa's all-rounder/left-arm medium pacer Trevor Goddard, whose ER of 1.64 is marginally better for his 123 wickets in 41 Tests—the same number of Tests as Nadkarni's. Durani, by contrast, had an ER of 2.47. Durani's ER places him eleventh among Indian bowlers, the top 10 not surprisingly all being spinners.

Together they were the perfect foil, Nadkarni bottling one side up with his flat, defensive line, and Durani flighting it and always attacking the batsman with his sharp turn and bounce. They took over the mantle of the spinning all-rounder from the immortal Vinoo Mankad, who played 44 Tests between 1946 and 1959 and who, at his peak, was acknowledged along with Australia's Keith Miller as the world's leading all-rounder. But so mighty were Mankad's contributions that it took the combination of both Nadkarni and Durani playing together to attempt to match his feats. Mankad remains the only cricketer in Test history to take eight wickets in an innings twice as well as score two double centuries, both as opener.

Sujit Mukherjee in his own delightful way wrote how both left-arm spinners were so often played in the same XI, 'The difficulty in having to choose between Durani and Nadkarni was solved, in the manner of the Union Government, by retaining both in the eleven.'[94] Mukherjee is referring here to the 1961–62 series against England but this trend continued. He also contrasted their bowling styles, 'The impetuous Durani attacked the batsmen all the time [...] His surreptitious nip off the wicket enabled him to obtain sudden turn and lift to surprise the batsmen [...] Nadkarni's bowling was motivated by an instinct for thrift [...] which made him concentrate on an undriveable patch on unvarying length about three inches outside off stump to right-handed batsmen.'[95] Mukherjee also compares their strongly contrasted batting styles to their bowling and puts both down to their two 'very dissimilar personalities'.

Indian cricket may have historically produced a paucity of left-handed batsmen but that has not been the case with left-arm bowlers and particularly all-leftie all-rounders—Nadkarni, Durani, Rusi Surti, Eknath Solkar, Karsan Ghavri, Irfan Pathan and Ravindra Jadeja—those who both batted and bowled left. Of these, Surti, Solkar and Ghavri, though mainly medium pacers, could all turn to spin when warranted. Even more unusual was that in eight Tests, including all five in West Indies in 1962, India had three all-lefties—Nadkarni, Durani and Surti—in their playing XI. Mankad incidentally bowled left and batted right, as did Ravi Shastri.

The Riot

In retrospect, Durani may perhaps have been relieved at having missed the Calcutta Test as it witnessed one of the worst riots

---

[94]Mukherjee, Sujit, *Playing for India*, Orient Longman, Hyderabad, 1988, p. 236.
[95]Ibid.

in cricket history. On the opening day, West Indies crawled to 212 for four after winning the toss. Things got out of hand the next day: New Year's Day 1967. An estimated 80,000 thronged the ground, thousands of them with forged or duplicate tickets allegedly sold on the black market. Even before a ball had been bowled, the crowd grew restive as it spilled over the stands and across the boundary lines.

The fuse was lit when the police brutally beat up a spectator by the name of Sitesh Roy, who had been pleading with them to exercise restraint. Infuriated, the crowd now turned on the police. Heavily outnumbered, they were forced to beat a hasty retreat even as lathis and tear gas-shells rained down. It was utter pandemonium with the players fleeing to what they thought was the safety of the pavilion—which was then set on fire. Charlie Griffith and other West Indians, in blind panic and fearing for their lives, fled to their hotel that was barely a kilometre away. As bamboo poles were uprooted and shamianas set on fire, the pitch was also vandalized and the violence spread outside the stadium with buses and police vehicles set ablaze.

The players were left unharmed—the ire of the crowd was not directed at them. When the Indians scrambled into the team bus that would take them back to the Great Eastern Hotel, they found to their shock a bunch of CAB officials cowering under their seats, pleading to be saved from the lynch mob. Reportedly, the chairman of selectors was among them.

Not a ball was bowled that day and the next was declared a rest day, which normally came after three days of play back then. Meanwhile, hectic meetings were held between the teams, the West Bengal state and police officials, as well as BCCI and CAB officials. It was the Indian team's local manager, Dilip Ghosh, of the Gymkhana Club, who persuaded Sir Frank Worrell to intervene.

The former captain was Dean of Students at the University of West Indies (St Augustine Campus, Trinidad and Tobago Division) and was on a lecture tour of India organized by the University Grants Commission (UGC). He made it clear to Sobers and his men that abandoning the Test and the tour would have serious repercussions. He also reminded them of similar incidents back home though not quite this serious. Just three months later, Worrell (42) would die of leukemia.

Pataudi and his men meanwhile caved in under pressure. They were told that if the Test and tour was called off, no foreign side would ever visit India again and Indian cricket would be irreparably harmed. The captain himself was convinced that the damage to the pitch would doom them to defeat since it would assist West Indies' bowlers. But he had no choice.

For their pains, the Indians were given ₹100 each—it was like adding insult to injury and sure enough, the home side succumbed by an innings in four days. The match continued without a hitch almost as if the riot had never happened. The ground staff did a miraculous job in clearing up the debris but there was nothing they could have done in the little time they had to repair the vandalized pitch.

As nominal editor of the now-defunct weekly *Sportsworld*, Pataudi wrote about the incident with the sensationalist and somewhat misleading heading, 'When India Was Asked to Lose a Test'.[96] But one gets the gist. Gibbs and Sobers had seven wickets each and the series was now won and lost. As for debutant Bedi: he claimed the wickets of Basil Butcher and Lloyd and that was enough to impress his captain, with whom he forged a life-long bond till the latter's death in 2011. The third Test at Madras was drawn but not before the visitors had survived a scare. So the home side acquitted itself reasonably well.

---

[96]'When India Was Asked to Lose a Test', *Sportsworld*, 6 January 1982.

Once the series was over, the focus was back on the domestic scene. The Ranji Trophy had become almost predictable by now—yes, Bombay versus Rajasthan in the final for the sixth time in seven years, and Bombay retaining the title. This time, though, there was no outright victory. The match was drawn but Bombay's massive first innings lead was enough. Durani had nothing to show, though in the semi-final against Bengal he had five wickets and also scored a century and 95 in the league phase. The final at Bombay itself was lit up by a century and double century by Rajasthan's brilliant captain Hanumant Singh. But, as usual for Rajasthan, it was not enough.

Hanumant made it to the team to England in 1967 but, with the spin quartet touring for the first time, there was no place for either Nadkarni or Durani. The senior of the two had toured England in 1959 but for Durani it was a huge disappointment to miss out again. India were beaten in all three Tests having lost all five on the previous tour.

It was the Duleep Trophy and the Irani Cup which were the basis for selection of the Indian team to Australia and New Zealand in 1967–68. In the event, Durani had just one match to impress as Central were eliminated by South Zone in the Duleep semi-final at Bangalore. He was a shock omission from the Rest of India side for the Irani Cup against Bombay which followed, and which was the final match before the team announcement. Durani scored 61 and 14 for Central, bowled 17 wicket-less overs, and that was it. His name did not figure in the touring squad, though Nadkarni was back after being omitted for the England tour.

A Devastating Blow

This was a devastating blow, one that sent Durani into a spiral of depression. Utterly dejected by his continued omission from the national side, he made himself unavailable for Rajasthan in the 1967–68 Ranji Trophy season. That was a major factor in the runners-up of the last two seasons failing to advance beyond the zonal stage. By retaining their title for the tenth consecutive time, Bombay bettered the previous record for a domestic team, New South Wales in Australia's Sheffield Shield between 1953–54 and 1961–62. They would stretch it to 15 in a row in 1972–73 before losing in the 1973–74 semi-final to Karnataka.

In a tribute to him after his death, the veteran journalist and Durani's old friend Prakash Bhandari quoted him about how shattered he was by the rejection. 'When I was not included in the Indian team to tour Australia in 1967, [and New Zealand in 1968; it was a twin-tour] I was a broken man. It was during this phase Raj Singh-ji helped me by boosting my morale, helping me overcome my domestic and personal problems, helping me financially. I was doomed, but Raj-bhai helped me a lot and even gave me a place to live [...] when I was broke and jobless.'[97]

The series in New Zealand marked the final one for Nadkarni. The standout performer of the twin tours was Surti, who had also caught the eye of the Queensland selectors. He decided eventually to emigrate to Australia, where he became the first Indian to compete in the domestic Sheffield Shield competition.

With no international cricket at home in 1968–69, Durani had no choice but to plug on in the domestic circuit. Back for Rajasthan after missing the previous season, it was the team's misfortune that this time they faced the invincible Bombay in the semi-final rather than the usual final. The result was no different, though Durani with 85 and 74 showed he was still a

---

[97]Bhandari, Prakash, 'I Would Have Been the King of Limited Overs Cricket', http://tinyurl.com/5n6t59mh, *rediff.com*, 7 April 2023. Accessed on 17 April 2023.

class apart. This time it was the turn of Bengal to fall to Bombay in the final. Durani's repeated omission from the Rest of India XI in the Irani Cup continued to baffle. It was the traditional curtain-raiser to the domestic season and notable performances carried considerable weight with the national selectors. The last occasion he had played the vital tie was in the 1965–66 season.

New Zealand and Australia returned the favour of the 1967–68 twin tour when they came to India in 1969–70 for three and five Tests, respectively. The Indian performance was below par and so was the batting form of Pataudi. India were fortunate to draw 1–1 with the Kiwis, but were beaten 3–1 by a strong Australian side led by Bill Lawry. By now Bedi had firmly established himself in the team. But with three spinners with few pretensions to batting and a couple of bits-and-pieces medium-paced all-rounders in the XI, the Indian tail was far too long. With eight Tests ahead over the two series, this was the ideal opportunity for Durani to force his way back in.

It did not happen. And this, despite putting in an impressive performance for Central Zone against the Aussies at Jaipur between the first Test at Bombay (which India lost) and the drawn second at Kanpur. This series followed the one against New Zealand which had begun in September 1969. Before the Kiwis began their three Tests, the domestic season started early with the Irani Cup—no Durani as usual—and the Duleep Trophy in which he failed to impress in Central's two games.

The Aussies' Jaipur tour match was the first to be staged at the half-completed Sawai Mansingh Stadium in Jaipur before his adoring fans. This is what Rajan Bala wrote in his account of the tours, 'I had a talk with Durani [before the match]. What he said doesn't matter and would surely get him into trouble with the Board but that is Durani—outspoken and prone to indiscretion. If he hadn't both "qualities" possibly this wayward genius would have been winning more Tests for India, instead of kicking his heels in obscurity. The all-rounder seemed determined to do well [...] but lapsed into despondency with the remark, "that won't fetch me a place in the Test side." Why? That is a question that everyone has been asking.'[98]

Bala had summed up Durani's mood well. He described his innings of 55 and 33 as superb and wrote, 'He bowled really well though his figures [24-3-65-2] did not tell the story.' One remarkable part of that story was when a ball from Durani grazed the stumps of the tourists' best batsman Doug Walters but did not disturb the bails. 'To see Walters who played a great knock of 84 beaten at full stretch forward, with a delivery which spun past a lunging bat was a sight for the gods. Durani smiled with contempt, swept back an unruly lock of hair and continued with an almost stoic indifference,' wrote Bala.[99] Durani did eventually get Walters' prized wicket and also that of Jock Irvine.

Australia won by an innings and 32 runs. But the honours belonged to the luckless Durani whose gloomy prediction to Bala proved sadly correct. He did not gain a place in the national team for any of the eight home Tests.

Chairman of selectors Vijay Merchant announced that he was going for youth for the 1969–70 Tests. Youngsters were chosen all right—Ashok Gandotra, Ajit Pai, Ambar Roy—but they came and went with alarming regularity. Here a quote from Durani's contemporary, left-arm spinner Dilip Doshi, who toiled for many years for Bengal (and in county cricket in England) before gaining a belated Test call-up in 1979–80, is apt. 'Salim Durani was the most wasted genius cricketer that I have ever seen in India. The weakness of Indian cricket then

---

[98]Bala, Rajan, *Kiwis and Kangaroos, India 1969*, The Statesman Press, Calcutta, 1970, p. 84.
[99]Ibid

was it failed to recognize Salim-bhai's true genius—and I don't use that word very often.'[100]

It was cold comfort but Rajasthan did make it to the Ranji final in 1969–70—with predictable results. Yes, for the seventh time in 10 seasons, starting from 1960–61, they finished on the losing side to Bombay. Eight wickets in the quarter-final versus Railways, and six in the semi-final versus Bengal saw Durani nicely warmed up for the final—and a desperate hope and prayer that Rajasthan would finally turn the tables on Bombay.

It was not to be. Bombay were back in their lion's den of Brabourne. The only thing falling in favour of the visitors was the coin. Once they were dismissed for 217 on the opening day, it was just a matter of time before the mighty Bombay batting machine ground their bowlers into the dust. The massive total of 531 meant Bombay only had to bat once, winning by an innings and 59 runs. This was in fact the third time in the seven finals between the two that Bombay had won by an innings—a measure of just how vast the gulf was between the best and second best in the country.

Durani at least had the consolation of picking up four wickets including the top three in the batting order—Sunil Gavaskar (a year away from his fabled Test career), Ashok Mankad and Wadekar. Gavaskar's 114 was his first century in the national championships. It was enough to drive a man to drink—or as in the case of Durani, to poetry.

'*Hazaaron khwahishen aisi ke har khwahish pe dam nikley, bohot nikley mere armaan, lekin phir bhi kam nikle* [Thousands of desires, each worth dying for ... many of them I have realized, yet I yearn for more],' Durani said, quoting the opening lines of a poem by Mirza Ghalib when interviewed in 2012 on the

---

[100]Gollapudi, Nagraj, 'Spin Bowling Is a Battle of Wits', *Cricinfo Magazine*, February 2006.

occasion of Rajasthan finally achieving what they had failed to do back in the 1960s—win the Ranji Trophy not once, but twice in succession.[101]

Rajasthan's Achilles' heel was its fielding. Catches were dropped with alarming regularity, including Gavaskar's twice on the way to his maiden Ranji 100. They went through a procession of mediocre wicketkeepers including Durani himself as a stop-gap for one season and Parthasarthi 'Parath' Sharma, a middle order batsman who played five Tests and was a liability anywhere in the field.

Sharma in particular was all at sea while keeping to Durani, dropping catches galore and fumbling stumpings, infuriating the bowler though he never showed his irritation on the field. Durani's record would have been so much better had even half these chances been taken. It was not till the discovery of Sunil Benjamin, ironically by Sharma himself, that Rajasthan finally found a safe pair of hands behind the stumps. Benjamin, who came from an impoverished background, played 70 Ranji games for Rajasthan over 16 seasons.

The bowling was in the capable hands of pace bowler Kailash Gattani and leg spinner C.G. 'Chandu' Joshi, apart from Durani. Gattani was distinctly unlucky not to make it to the national side at the time when spin bowling was dominant. Joshi taught art and sculpture at the prestigious Mayo College in Ajmer. They are the only surviving members of that glorious period of Rajasthan cricket. Joshi, now 91 and living in Pune, was briefly appointed as Durani's tutor by Bhagwat Singh who was determined the young Salim pass his Matriculation, but to no avail. Gattani saw things differently. Now running a coaching

---

[101]Purohit, Abhishek, 'When Seven Finals in Ten Years Was Not Enough', *ESPNcricinfo*, 22 January 2012, http://tinyurl.com/4d5h937r. Accessed on 3 May 2023.

camp in Pune, he told me that in batting, bowling and fielding, Bombay were superior back then and all else were merely excuses. Rajasthan did well in reaching the finals all those years but Bombay were just too formidable.

'They were full-time cricketers, younger and fitter. They played tournaments throughout the year while Rajasthan were part-timers, many involved in business or other activities. While Bombay were busy playing or attending coaching camps all year in Rajasthan we would have short camps just before the finals. Fielding drills would include taking 100 catches but what is the use of these short camps when our opponents are 365 days-a-year professionals?'[102]

Ramachandra Guha, an ardent admirer of Durani, picked him (as well as Gattani) in his all-time Rajasthan XI. Restricting his selection only to those either born or domiciled in the state, this was his team in batting order: Suryaveer Singh, Laxman Singh, Hanumant Singh (captain), Parthasarthi Sharma, Salim Durani, Kishan Rungta, Sunil Benjamin (wicketkeeper), Kailash Gattani, Bhagwat Singh of Mewar, G.R. Sunderam and Chandu Joshi.[103]

The Prince and the Nawab

Tiger Pataudi was assigned by a publication with picking an all-time India XI. Assisting him was his dear friend, the sports official Amrit Mathur. 'You put in anyone you want, he told me, as long you have Salim's name there. Anyone who knew Tiger even remotely would confirm that was high praise. Tiger wasn't the type to get easily impressed.'[104]

---

[102]Conversation with author on 3 September 2023.
[103]Guha, Ramachandra, *Wickets in the East: An Anecdotal History*, Oxford University Press, New Delhi, 1992, p. 147.
[104]Mathur, Amrit, 'Chapter 5: Salim Durani', *My Cricket Hero: XII Indians on*

Between the Vinoo Mankad era of the 1940s and 50s, and the Kapil Dev era beginning in 1978, Durani was the only Indian cricketer to win Test matches for India with both bat and ball. Pataudi (in 15 Tests) was his third captain after G.S. Ramchand (one Test) and Nari Contractor (seven). His fourth was Ajit Wadekar, with six tests.

While Mansur Ali Khan was born into royalty, Durani had the aura of royalty and stood out in a Rajasthan side that had its fair share of blue bloods. No wonder he was known as Prince Salim by his fellow cricketers in dressing rooms around the country and by his countless legions of fans as well.

So why was it that the relationship between Prince Salim and Nawab *sahab* was so strained?

They had much in common—and yet were also so different. Both were good-looking men who had a large female fan following and played cricket to win, with panache and style. I previously listed the six Indian cricketers of the 1960s that shared these traits. Tiger and Durani were by far the most popular of the lot. Both had Afghan lineage—Salim's father was born in Kabul while the Pataudi royal family traced their roots back to Salamat Khan, who came to India from Afghanistan in 1480.[105]

Both their fathers played for India, though Tiger's father, Iftikhar, was much more famous, the only Test cricketer to represent both England and India, and captain the latter too. Stretching things a bit, both their wives (in Durani's case, his first) were in the movies. Tiger's wife, Sharmila Tagore, was of course the leading lady of Indian cinema when they married in 1968, while Salim's was a bit player. At least in one aspect, Durani was one up on Tiger—he acted in a movie, that too

---

Their XII Favourite Cricketers, Gulu Ezekiel (ed.), Rupa Publications, New Delhi, 2022, p. 37.

[105]Ezekiel, Gulu, 'Afghan Cricket: The Indian Connection', *rediff.com*, 27 June 2017, http://tinyurl.com/4t55kkx7. Accessed on 10 July 2023.

with Parveen Babi, no less! The Nawab no doubt would have turned his regal nose up at the very thought of emulating Prince Salim in this regard.

They both lost their fathers early, in a manner of speaking. While Mansur's father died of a heart attack on his son's eleventh birthday in 1952, Salim's walked out on the family when he was not much older than Mansur. They also enjoyed the good things in life, but Tiger could afford these luxuries and knew where to draw the line.

Yet, there were also so many differences about them. Tiger was born into immense wealth mainly due to his mother being from the Bhopal royal family and never having to work to earn a living. Durani, on the other hand, stumbled from one job to another, perennially broke and depending on friends, fans and family to see him through life. And while Tiger was one of the greatest captains produced by India, Durani always preferred to be led rather than lead. Tiger had the best of education in the poshest schools and colleges, while Salim was a school dropout.

An incident with Ian Chappell in Australia in 1967 when they met for the first time is an eye-opener. They had strong family connections: Chappell's grandfather Vic Richardson and Tiger's father Iftikhar Ali Khan were on opposing sides in the infamous Bodyline series in Australia in 1932–33 and both had an intense dislike of the English captain Douglas Jardine.

Intrigued by the royal presence, Chappell asked him what he did for a living. 'Ian, I'm a prince,' he replied, wrote Chappell. 'Not being familiar with the concept, I continued to prod him about what he did between the hours of nine to five. He became a little exasperated and said, "Ian, I'm a bloody prince." Still not grasping his meaning, I asked what he did when he went to the office. "Ian, I'm ****ing prince," was succinct enough, and in a language I understood, to get the message across.'[106]

Mind you, this was three years before Indian royalty were stripped of their titles and privy purses.

Tiger has gone on record that the only two teammates he had differences with were Borde and Durani. In Borde's case it was the feeling of resentment over the captaincy that always hovered over their relationship. Borde felt, by reasons of seniority, he should have been the one to lead the country in the long run rather than Tiger, who did so in 40 of his 46 Test matches.

But with Durani it was more to do with clashing temperaments as Tiger has emphasized in interviews over the years. Could this have been another reason for Durani's extended exile from the Test side? Back then, the captain did not sit in on selection committee meetings and Tiger was known to be laidback about such matters. But he always had the ear of the selectors and could put his foot down when insisting on a player being chosen—or not.

Case in point was G.R. Vishwanath. In his autobiography *Wrist Assured*, he narrates how, after being in the reserves, Tiger insisted he be included in the playing XI for the second Test at Kanpur against Australia in November 1969.[107] Merchant said he had never seen Vishwanath bat in a match, so how could he select him? Tiger replied he had seen him and that should be good enough, and the brilliant Vishy never looked back.

So what was the difficulty with Durani, whom Tiger acknowledged as a match-winner? Remember, it was during the period of Tiger's captaincy that Durani found himself out in the cold from 1967 to 1970—only to return in 1971 when

---

[106]Chappell, Ian, 'A Worldly-wise Larrikin', *Pataudi: Nawab of Cricket*, Suresh Menon (ed.), Harper Collins Publishers, Noida, 2013, p. 49.
[107]Vishwanath, Gundappa, with R. Kaushik, *Wrist Assured: An Autobiography*, Rupa Publications, New Delhi, 2022.

Pataudi was sacked and replaced by Wadekar.

This is what he said in an interview to Sambit Bal in *Wisden Asia Cricket* magazine, 'If he [a good captain] thinks the player has ability, it's his job to handle his personality. Every team has a couple of difficult characters [...] Salim Durani was one. I felt I couldn't handle him very well [...] Because I felt I couldn't get the best out of him. He was an extremely talented cricketer who lacked a certain amount of cricketing discipline [...] He did well, but a man of his talent could have been made to perform much better.'[108]

He was rather more frank with Rajan Bala. 'I made it a point to treat the players the same. As far as I am concerned, each has a role to play and if he did there was no bother. But it was beyond me to cajole someone to give his best. I know Jaisimha would do it. He was the one who was good in psychology. Salim probably needed a different sort of handling but then I had all sorts of players to contend with. If he had been more reasonable and realized and acted as a senior player there would have been a permanent place for him in the side. You would agree that it is up to the individual to make the best of the opportunities he gets. Probably I would not have treated Sobers, had he been playing for India, any differently.'[109]

The late journalist was a huge admirer of Pataudi. But he criticizes the absence of Durani from the 1967 tour of England, followed by Australia and New Zealand in 1967–68. 'Of course it was for the selection committee [...] to decide whether it needed Durani. It can be presumed that if his name did come up, Pataudi would not have been too enthusiastic,' wrote Bala. He added, 'I always felt that he never was able to utilise the

---

[108]Bal, Sambit, 'A Bad Captain Can Make a Great Team Look Ordinary', *Wisden Asia Cricket*, March 2002.
[109]Bala, Rajan, *The Covers Are Off: A Socio-Historical Study of Indian Cricket 1932-2003*, Rupa Publications, New Delhi, 2004, p. 119.

enormous talent of the whimsical Salim Durani.'[110]

Pataudi further said to Bala about Durani, 'There is no doubt that he is one of the most gifted cricketers that we have. But he is not better than Sobers. He probably does not understand how good he is. So he ends up being an underachiever. That is the worst thing for a talented person. I think he knows this too well, and hence plays up as being temperamental. In comparison, Nadkarni would be the last person to claim that he is inordinately gifted. But I could rely on him to do a specific job for the side. You cannot have prima donnas in the side.'[111]

It is clear that Pataudi preferred the safe Nadkarni to the flamboyant Durani in his side as the left-arm spinner/batsman option—which went against his generally positive attitude. It also goes against what he told Amrit Mathur. Nadkarni played 22 of his 41 Tests under Pataudi's captaincy, while Durani played 15 of his 29.

Certainly, when playing all those years for Rajasthan, his captains never expressed such reservations. In fact he had extremely warm relations with Bhagwat Singh Mewar, Raj Singh and Hanumant, who were his state captains. Durani must have been fed up with being asked by every journalist about his relationship with Pataudi. He generally met them with a straight diplomatic bat. He told Navneet Mundhra, 'As far as Pataudi is concerned, he was the best captain I played under. He was always aggressive and enterprising in his approach. Look, he had to manage not just me but 14 other cricketers as well, so he couldn't possibly channelise all his energy on me. I am solely, responsible for all my performances, good or otherwise.'[112]

---

[110]Ibid.
[111]Ibid. 112.
[112]Mundra, Navneet, 'Salim Durani – A Multi-Skilled Genius Who Would Have Been Perfect for IPL', *cricketcountry*, 26 April 2012, http://tinyurl.com/mr3fkj6j. Accessed on 11 April 2023.

He did, however, accept his weakness once in an interview with Ayaz Memon in *The Illustrated Weekly of India*, when asked about Pataudi. While rubbishing the 'rumours' of their rift, he admitted, 'I will not hesitate to confess that though I was talented, and a good teammate, I was a little temperamental. However, I was never guilty of indiscipline.'[113] Even Prasanna, who waxed eloquent about his 'genius' friend, accepted that much as he admired Durani, he had never captained him. 'Most of the captains under which Salim has played have made no secret that he is difficult to get along with. I haven't found him so. Of course I haven't led a side [...] He has his weaknesses, who does not?'[114]

This is what Ajit Wadekar, who was Durani's fourth and final Test captain, had to say about him, 'He never realized his full potential on this tour. [India in West Indies in 1971]. This temperamental all-rounder has cricket in his blood. But everything depends on his changing moods. He could win a match off his own bowling, or lose it by playing a wayward stroke when much was at stake.'[115]

Sunil Gavaskar had a different take from his first skipper. 'Salim has been a much misunderstood man. He has been called moody and this stigma has stuck to him. But this is not a correct estimate of the man [...] He is often accused of not taking Test cricket seriously. This is equally untrue [...] People call him a wayward genius. I don't know about his being wayward but he is certainly a genius. A genius whom the authorities have never bothered to understand.'[116]

Then again, as Prasanna wrote, he never captained Durani

---

[113] Memon, Ayaz, 'Mr Sixer', *The Illustrated Weekly of India*, March, 1991.
[114] Prasanna, E.A.S., *One More Over*, Rupa Publications, New Delhi, 1977, p. 83.
[115] Wadekar, Ajit, *My Cricketing Years*, Vikas Publishing House Pvt. Ltd, New Delhi, 1973, p. 35.
[116] Gavaskar, Sunil, *Sunny Days*, Rupa Publications, New Delhi, 1976, p. 251.

and neither did Gavaskar. Pataudi and Wadekar were among those who, at Test level, found him difficult to handle while at the same time acknowledging that he was a match-winner.

Mihir Bose adds an intriguing twist to this saga, 'The only cricketer to remotely threaten Tiger as a romantic hero, a personage both on and off the field, was Durani. The Salim-Pataudi relationship was complex and interesting.'[117] Bose draws a contrast between Tiger being held in awe due to his royal background while Durani was 'everyone's *yaar* (friend)', the favourite of the common man both for his rakish good looks and charm as well as his attacking batting and connection with the fans in the stands.[118] He adds, 'By then [1971, when Durani returned], Pataudi was gone and replaced by Wadekar and nothing could comfort Indian cricket for the lost years of Durani. This loss meant that one of the most charismatic cricketers India has produced never toured England, or Australia [...] However, he never lost the permanent hold he had gained in the hearts of Indian cricket followers of the 1960s.'[119]

Durani was generous in his tribute to Pataudi after his passing. 'He was dynamic, young and a perfect leader. After all, his background was such that he was destined to be a leader. Although he came from a royal background, he didn't have any ego issues. He always made sure that his stature didn't come in the way of friendship. *Nawab sahib zameen par bhi baith jate.* (Nawab sahib even sat on the floor.)'[120]

---

[117]Bose, Mihir, *The Nine Waves: The Extraordinary Story of Indian Cricket*, Aleph Book Company, New Delhi, 2019, p. 113.
[118]Ibid.
[119]Bose, Mihir, *A Maidan View: The Magic of Indian Cricket*, Penguin Books, New Delhi, 2006, p. 275.
[120]Vivek, G.S., 'Dynamic, Young and a Born Leader', *The Indian Express*, 23 September 2011.

Whether Pataudi or Dutta Ray, or even both of them in part, was responsible for Durani's unjust exile or not is open to debate and conjecture. But the fact remains that it took a bizarre set of circumstances that would set in motion both their exits in January 1971, and in turn, a dramatic comeback for the man I dubbed 'Destiny's Child'.

Five

Back in the Fold (1970–71 to 1977–78)

Bob Dylan's song 'Simple Twist of Fate' comes to mind when we look back at the strange turn of events that saw Ajit Wadekar replace Tiger Pataudi as captain of the team to tour the West Indies in early 1971.

The Byzantine ways of BCCI politics have produced many bizarre tales before and since. But few could match the twists and turns that saw the absence of M. Dutta Ray (Bengal) from the BCCI selection committee meeting in Bombay on 8 January 1971. This meeting saw the ouster of Pataudi after a remarkable run of eight years and 36 Tests in charge, unprecedented in the annals of Indian cricket.

Dutta Ray's absence meant there were now four selectors: chairman Vijay Merchant (West), C.D. Gopinath (South), H.T. Dani (North) and M.M. Jagdale (Central). Gopinath and Jagdale were for retaining Pataudi while Dani and Merchant were for Wadekar. Dutta Ray was a sure bet for Pataudi too, but in his absence and with the votes split 2-2, it came down to Merchant using his chairman's casting vote to go with Wadekar.

The team was chosen four days later and with Dutta Ray and Pataudi both out of the equation, the path was cleared for Durani to make a remarkable comeback after spending over four years in the wilderness of the domestic circuit.

Durani was sitting outside Merchant's office as the meeting dragged on, pacing up and down, knowing this was his final chance to come back. Having got the good news, he could finally breathe easy and so could his countless fans. He was one of four chosen for their experience of the 1962 tour, the others being M.L. Jaisimha, Dilip Sardesai and E.A.S. Prasanna. Wadekar made it clear to Merchant he wanted some old hands to guide him in his first series as captain and maiden tour of the Caribbean.

But what was behind the mysterious absence of the omnipotent Dutta Ray? Therein lies a tale.

The BCCI meeting in Madras on 28 October 1969 had produced a surprise in the defeat of Dutta Ray at the hands of former Test all-rounder Dattu Phadkar, who had settled in Calcutta. It was a close contest and it took the casting vote of BCCI President Zal Irani to break the deadlock in Phadkar's favour. After an unprecedented stint of 18 years as a national selector, Dutta Ray was stunned to find himself on the sidelines and vowed to make a comeback. Irani's term over, it was now A.N. Ghose of Bengal who became president. Sure enough, a year later, Dutta Ray was back in the national selection panel after the BCCI meeting in New Delhi on 30 September 1970. He had spent the past 11 months lobbying to return and was now joined by Jagdale, making it five selectors including Chairman Merchant.

Dutta Ray was a polarizing figure and was not popular with an influential section of the BCCI. But he gave a written undertaking to his old friend from Calcutta, the new president Ghose, that if re-elected, he would resign within 60 days—30 November 1970 being the deadline. For Dutta Ray only wished to make a point—that he was all-powerful and could not be ousted for long.

Wily as a fox, Dutta Ray, once he got his foot back in the door, would not step aside unless pushed. However, he antagonized even his own backers by lobbying for Keki Tarapore as manager for West Indies when the consensus candidate was Col Hemu Adhikari. Tarapore won the vote on 6 January by a narrow 11–9 margin thanks to Dutta Ray's machinations. But now he had burned his bridges within the Board and his opponents were determined he could not extend his 60-day promise, though he tried every trick in the book to stay on till the two selection committee meetings on 8 and 12 January.

This time though, the master wheeler-dealer had met his match. While earlier even his antagonists were willing to look the other way and ignore his resignation deadline, they now put up a united front to oppose him following the controversial manager's selection. Eleven out of 27 voting members wrote to Ghose insisting Dutta Ray's role as selector should be terminated—they threatened legal action otherwise. Ghose had no choice but to accede to their demand and Dutta Ray beat a hasty retreat back to Calcutta, with Ghose claiming he was suffering from 'high blood pressure', hence could not attend the two vital meetings.

Back in Calcutta, Dutta Ray attempted to vote by proxy. Merchant though was firm this would not be allowed as it went against the Board's own constitution—all selectors had to be physically present in order to participate in the debate. Merchant also stood up to pressure exerted by Ghose to postpone the meetings to allow Dutta Ray to 'recover'.

Recover from what? Who should pop up at the BCCI's Special General Meeting in Madras on 13 January but Dutta Ray himself, apparently in the pink of health—just 24 hours after the meeting in Bombay to select the team! And he was adamant that he had not resigned.

What is remarkable is Dutta Ray not only survived his apparent health scare and the plot to have him thrown out, he was still on the committee in June 1971 when the team to tour

England was selected, keeping his slot till 1971–72. But then, in the murky world of Indian sports administration, such Machiavellian acts were far from unknown. Durani was in outstanding all-round form for Vazir Sultan Tobacco XI in the Moin-ud-Dowlah Gold Cup tournament in Hyderabad, for Rajasthan in the Ranji Trophy Central Zone league, and for Central Zone in the Duleep Trophy as the 1970–71 season got underway. But what really caught the eye of the selectors was his century for Rest of India versus Ranji Trophy champions Bombay in the Irani Cup match at Eden Gardens in December 1970.

It was only the second time after 1965–66 that Durani was chosen for this prestigious match which carried immense weight back then. His exclusion from the Rest of India team in the interim period was baffling and placed him at a severe disadvantage when it was time to select the Indian team.

This was now a crunch match for Durani. For all practical purposes it was a trial match for the West Indies tour and he knew he had to come good if he was to get this chance for national honours after such a long gap. And come good he did. Though he failed to take a single wicket in the 21 overs he bowled in the match, his century came close to giving Rest the first innings lead. Unusually for Durani, he buckled down to play a sedate knock, perhaps realizing how high the stakes were. He batted for 262 minutes and hit 16 boundaries but rarely lofted the ball.

The storm over Pataudi's sacking and the exclusion of Farokh Engineer and Rusi Surti meant Durani's comeback slipped under the radar. Engineer (Lancashire) and Surti (Queensland) were not eligible for selection under a new and short-lived rule of the BCCI whereby Indians playing abroad had to play a full domestic season in India to stand a chance for selection. This also caused a furore and, sure enough, Engineer was back for the three Tests that followed later that year in England. Surti's exclusion was certainly a lucky break for Durani, as he now took the all-rounder's slots with Eknath Solkar and Syed Abid Ali.

The other point of interest was the selection of Bombay opener Sunil Gavaskar for his maiden series. At 21, he was the baby of the squad. By the end of the series, he would emerge the giant.

Gone with the Windies

As for West Indies, they were a team in transition. The once-mighty side of the 1960s was going through a lean patch with the retirement of some of their batting stalwarts and the fading away of the fast bowling terrors Wes Hall and Charlie Griffith. Captain Garry Sobers was also feeling the strain of non-stop cricket both at the international level and domestically in West Indies and England. After winning his first three Test series as captain from 1964-65 to 1966-67, West Indies, under his captaincy, after the 1966-67 tour of India, had lost three and drawn one of their last four series. It had been nine years since India's traumatic tour of 1962, one of the most disastrous in cricket history, and now they had a captain untested at international level.

The tour did not start well. Gavaskar had an infected finger that needed emergency surgery in New York en-route Kingston, Jamaica, and Vishwanath's painful knee was yet to heal. The opening match against Jamaica at Sabina Park was drawn with the Indians not being particularly impressive against a weak team that contained only two Test cricketers in Maurice Foster and captain Easton McMorris. There was also a young superstar in the making, batsman Lawrence Rowe, as well as leg spinner Arthur Barrett, wicketkeeper Desmond Lewis and fast bowler Uton Dowe, all of whom would go on to make their Test debuts in the series.

It was Durani who was the first century maker of the tour for the Indians with 131 (with 21 boundaries) in the second innings. He also scored a useful 34 in the first. It was the veteran Sardesai who just missed on the distinction, run out for 97 in the first innings. Gavaskar gave a vivid description in *Sunny Days*, 'Durani played as only he can. With a minimum movement of his feet he still got the maximum power behind his shots which fairly sizzled over the grass. He hooked Dowe out of the small Sabina Park ground and then cover-drove him to the boundary. This caused excitement among the tree-top spectators, who began to jump and clap with such gusto that a branch of the tree crashed down with its human load.'[121]

Unfortunately, Durani suffered a hairline fracture in the little finger of his right hand. It was eerily similar to his finger injury on the eve of his Test debut in Bombay in January 1960, though that was on his left bowling hand. But he soldiered on and played the next two warm-up games as well, though the injury hampered his batting and he was perhaps fortunate to play in the opening Test at Kingston. The day before the Test, Wadekar asked him if he was fit to play and Durani, not wanting to jeopardize his chance after such a long lay-off, answered in the affirmative. Not allowing the finger to heal meant his batting was severely affected but it was a risk he was willing to take. After all, he could still bowl.

The first Test at Kingston, Jamaica, was a topsy-turvy one. The entire first day was washed out reducing it to a four-day Test. Put in to bat by Sobers, India crashed to 75 for five with only Sardesai left standing among the ruins of the top order. The opening bowlers, Vanburn Holder and Grayson Shillingford, had done the damage and it looked like the script of the 5–0 drubbing of 1962 was going to repeat itself.

---

[121]Gavaskar, Sunil, *Sunny Days*, Rupa Publications, New Delhi, 1976, p. 36.

Now came another twist as Sardesai's Bombay teammate Solkar (61) batted valiantly in the first overseas Test of his fledgling career to record his maiden Test 50. Batting for a shade over three hours, Solkar's stand with Sardesai was worth 137 and pulled the innings out of the mire. With Sardesai gallantly holding the fort, the tail wagged furiously and India's total of 387 was a tremendous display of fighting spirit which would hold them in good stead throughout the series. Sardesai batted half-an-hour short of 500 minutes—his marathon innings of 212 was the first double century by an Indian on foreign soil. And to think he was an eleventh-hour inclusion only on the insistence of his skipper.

West Indies were cruising along and the fourth wicket did not fall till 183. Then the spin trio of Bishan Bedi, vice captain S. Venkataraghavan and Prasanna got to work, bowling all but 11 overs of the 93.5 in the innings as the last seven wickets tumbled for a miserable 34 runs—217 all out. India's lead was 170.

That's when the astute Venkat pulled a rabbit out of the hat. It was the vice captain who informed Wadekar that, with no play on the first day and the Test now reduced to four days, the follow on target, too, was reduced from the conventional 200 runs to 150. (This is only the case when there is no play specifically on the first day.) The story of Venkat's crucial role has circulated for years. But is it true? This is what he told Aditya Bhushan, 'Not a story, it's a fact. In those days, as a player, I used to take so much interest in reading the rules. I used to know the laws of the game from top to bottom.'[122] No wonder Venkat, post-retirement, became the only Indian Test cricketer to qualify as a Test umpire.

---

[122]Aditya, Bhushan, and Sachin Bajaj, *Fortune Turners: The Quartet That Spun India to Glory*, Global Cricket School, Mumbai, 2019, p. 94.

Though the hosts' batting in the follow on easily saw out the draw, the psychological impact and indeed humiliation of following on against India for the first time since the maiden series in 1948–49 was incalculable. Wadekar and his men on the other hand felt vindicated after being brushed off as not much better than a club side by some of the locals early on in the tour. Though Durani did nothing of note at Kingston, he did enough to hold his place for the second Test at Port of Spain, Trinidad, thanks to useful all-round performances in the two games between the first and second Tests.

That Magic Spell

With its large 'East Indian' population packing the stands, the Queen's Park Oval has always been like a home-away-from-home for the Indian team. And, sure enough, this was the venue where they finally put it over West Indies in the twenty-fifth Test between the two teams. It marked the debut of opener Gavaskar, who had by now recovered from the finger infection and his impact on the series was immediate with 65 and 67 not out on debut, as India won by seven wickets.

There was a familiar script as the first Test except Sobers chose to bat this time after winning the toss. West Indies batting once again failed to click and once again India gained a big lead—214 all out as against India's 352. Sardesai had the highest score (112) and Solkar had another 50—all uncannily similar to the first Test.

By the end of the third day, West Indies had wiped off the deficit of 138 runs for the loss of only Rohan Kanhai's wicket. At 150 for one, with Roy Fredericks batting on 80 and Charlie Davis on 33, it looked like the pendulum had swung away from India.

But two injuries dramatically changed the course of events. Prasanna hurt his spinning finger in attempting a caught and bowled from Fredericks and was out of action for the fourth day. And a stroke of ill luck meant that Davis too could not bat on resumption—and Fredericks was the 'culprit'.

The two overnight batsmen were practising in adjacent nets on the fourth morning before start of play when a ferocious square cut from Fredericks tore through a hole in the netting and struck Davis over the eye. He had to be taken to hospital for seven stitches and his place at the crease in the morning was taken by Clive Lloyd.

The first over of the day was bowled by Venkat to Lloyd, a maiden. Seemingly disturbed by his inadvertent part in the unfortunate mishap, Fredericks was run out without adding to his overnight 80 in the second over of the day bowled by Durani—Prasanna was out of action after bowling 16 overs on the third day.

The opener hit the bowler to cover point where substitute K. Jayantilal fielding for Sardesai collected and threw the ball in smartly to wicketkeeper P. Krishnamurthy. It was an impossible run and Fredericks could not regain his crease after being sent back by Lloyd—150 for two. Sobers then stepped into the breach with Davis still nursing his injury. Now two left-handers were at the crease, the captain and Lloyd. What happened next became a vivid chapter in the tapestry of Indian cricket's history.

The mighty Sobers playing his fifteenth Test and twenty-fourth innings against India had an awesome record and had never been out against India without scoring. But there is always a first time and it was none other than Durani who was responsible for the great man's ignominy at a crucial point in the Test and series.

Fredericks was run out in the fifty-eighth over of the innings; the next bowled by Venkat saw Lloyd take two. Now in the sixtieth of the innings and fourth of the day, it was Durani versus Sobers—left-handers both. For the first five balls of the over, Sobers pushed and prodded—he was all at sea as Durani bowling round the wicket held him on a tight leash. Sobers hated being tied down, his pride and attacking instincts just could not accept a bowler dictating terms to him. Perhaps he, too, underestimated Durani's skills.

The final ball of the over did the trick.

In Durani's words, 'After pitching some deliveries outside off to Garry, I pitched one on this rough spot just outside the off stump. It hit the spot nicely, turned a little, beat his defence, went between bat and pad and took the off stump. He couldn't believe it and walked back muttering, "Oh Jesus." I couldn't control my happiness and was jumping in jubilation.'[123]

K.N. Prabhu, reporting for *The Times of India*, described it thus, 'It pitched on a length that pins the batsman to his crease and draws the tentative stroke. It broke to clip the off bail [...] Sobers had no stroke [...]'[124] Wadekar called it a dream delivery and, in the same interview with Gollapudi, compared it to Shane Warne's so-called 'ball of the century' that bowled Mike Gatting in 1993. Unfortunately, with no television footage available, it cannot be viewed by millions.

Seventeen runs later, Lloyd (15) was sent back, another master ball by Durani and a master stroke by Wadekar. Venkat and Durani were bowling in tandem and getting assistance from the turning track to tie down the batsmen. While Sobers was dismissed in Durani's second over, he got Lloyd's wicket in his sixth. From 150 for one, overnight the hosts in the span of 12 overs had plunged to 169 for four. The very next over it was 169 for five when the tireless Venkat bowled Steve Camacho for three.

---

[123]Gollapudi, Nagaraj, 'The Indian Public Had Been Hungry for a Victory of This Kind for Long', *The Cricket Monthly*, 21 December 2008, http://tinyurl.com/yd5sehn5. Accessed on 27 July 2023.
[124]Prabhu, K.N., 'Team Work Gives India First-Ever Win over W. Indies', *The Times of India*, 11 March 1971.

Wrote Wadekar, 'Noticing Lloyd pushing balls that broke into him towards mid-wicket, I moved over to short mid-wicket. I had barely taken up the position when Lloyd, as expected, hit the ball to me. I had to reach out and reclaim it, almost off my fingertips.'[125]

This was Durani's description, 'There was a little rough outside the off-stump of Lloyd. I tried to take the ball out in the air (drift) and break it into him. He was beaten in the flight and he hit the ball with the spin into the hands of Wadekar at short mid-wicket. It was a great catch by Wadekar.'[126]

'The wicket was slow and unresponsive to the flighted deliveries of Bedi, so they needed someone like me to hit the deck and make it spin. I also had the ability to vary the pace and that added another dimension to my bowling,' Durani told authors S. Giridhar and V.J. Raghunath.[127]

Davis came back and batted courageously for 74 not out to add to his 71 not out in the first innings. But it was not enough as Windies were all out for 261. India reached the victory target of 124 for the loss of three wickets, with debutant Gavaskar fittingly hitting the winning runs. Venkat bowled manfully to return the best figures of 36-11-95-5, while Bedi picked up two wickets. But all those present—Indian and West Indian journalists and players on both sides—agreed it was those two priceless wickets by Durani that turned the tide. His figures were 17-8-21-2.

Wrote the doyen of West Indian cricket journalists, the late Tony Cozier, 'Venkataraghavan, the off spinner, ended with

---

[125]Wadekar, Ajit, *My Cricketing Years*, Vikas Publishing House Pvt. Ltd, Delhi, 1973, p. 71.

[126]Viswanath, G., 'Salim Durani: Was So Overjoyed When I Bowled Garry Sobers', *Sportstar*, 10 March 2021, http://tinyurl.com/5ym2zshv. Accessed on 14 April 2023.

[127]Giridhar, S., and V.J. Raghunath, *From Mumbai to Durban: India's Greatest Tests*, Juggernaut Books, New Delhi, 2016, p. 71.

five wickets but it was Durani, the left hander, who struck the most telling blows [...]'[128] The three Indian journalists present, the UK-based Dicky Rutnagur, Berry Sarbadhikary and K.N. Prabhu, all concurred with Cozier.

There were a lot of outstanding performers in this famous victory, the first time West Indies had lost to India who were so ably led by Wadekar in only his second Test in charge. It might seem a tad unfair then to claim Durani as the real match-winner. After all he had just two wickets in the match and had scores of nine and zero. But those were special wickets and it took special deliveries to claim them. No wonder his feat at Port of Spain is written in letters of gold in the annals of Indian cricket.

The genesis of those two breakthroughs in fact occurred in the captain's hotel room the night before. It took a combination of Durani's chutzpah, Jaisimha's game sense and Wadekar's open mind in plotting the downfall of Sobers and Lloyd the next morning. And once again Destiny's Child was in the thick of things.

The fact is if Prasanna had been able to bowl on the fourth (and what turned out to be, final) day, then it is highly unlikely Durani would have got an extended spell first thing in the morning. After all, in the first innings Prasanna was India's best bowler with four for 54 and bowled 16 overs in the second before injury struck. Durani, by contrast, did not bowl a single over in the first innings with the spin trio claiming eight of the 10 wickets.

Like Venkat and the declaration incident from the Kingston Test, there are various versions of the Jaisimha-Durani-Wadekar story as well. Understandable, really, when you consider how many years passed before some of the interviews were conducted, 50-plus years in some cases.

---

[128]Cozier, Tony, 'India Go One Up', *The Cricketer*, May 1971.

Piecing things together, this much is clear: Durani confidently told Jaisimha he would get both the batsmen out the next day if given the ball by the skipper. Jaisimha, who was part of the team's brains trust but had been dropped for the Port of Spain Test, conveyed this to Wadekar in his room in the presence of Durani, Prasanna and Vishwanath.

It speaks volumes about Wadekar's lack of ego that he was happy to consult the seniors on tour. Vishwanath was obviously a fan. This is what he wrote in his autobiography on the tour, 'Ajit was a phenomenal leader who played a big part in our emergence as a strong Test force. He was an excellent batsman in his own right, and his man-management skills were exemplary [...] Ajit didn't impose himself, nor was he insecure when surrounded by such giants as Jai [Jaisimha]. It spoke of the spirit within the group that everyone pulled in the same direction [...]'[129]

10 March 1971 was a golden day in the history of Test cricket. But there were still three Tests remaining. Could India clinch the rubber?

The injury to Prasanna meant he was ruled out for the third and fourth Tests. The Bourda pitch at Georgetown, Guyana, was a placid one, and with both sides packed with batsmen, it ended in a bore-draw. Durani got his lone wicket of opener Joey Carew in the first innings, but he was involved in an incident that brought out the frustrations of the Indians against the umpires.

Durani was convinced he had Sobers caught at short leg by Sardesai off bat and pad in the second innings when he was on only one. The appeal was turned down by umpire Cecil Kippins, and the enraged Durani screamed another appeal even

---

[129]Vishwanath, Gundappa, with R. Kaushik, *Wrist Assured: An Autobiography*, Rupa Publications, New Delhi, 2022, p. 63.

as Sardesai flung the ball down in disgust. As the ball came near the bowler, he instinctively threw it at the non-striker's stumps. It narrowly missed the umpire, who accused Durani of trying to hit him with it. Fortunately, the incident blew over though it left the Indians enraged.

This is Wadekar's account, 'It was clear as daylight [...] There was no question of the fielder obscuring the umpire's view. Sobers did not walk, though there was no doubt the ball had curled off his defensive bat. Durani appealed twice in disgust.'[130]

Sobers had a reputation as one of the game's great gentlemen and was known to walk even before the umpire's verdict if he knew he was out. But he had been under pressure after the Port of Spain defeat and was still searching for his first century of the series—which he duly got thanks to this reprieve.

Wrote Gavaskar, 'I was fielding at long-on and I saw the deflection clearly and naturally jumped with joy in anticipation of our having taken the prize wicket of the great Sobers. But Garry waited and the umpire ruled not out. For once Salim Durani lost his cool [...] I don't blame him. He had started the tour brilliantly and was now on the verge of losing his Test place.'[131]

Even Tony Cozier was critical in *The Cricketer*, 'Sobers' effort, despite a glittering array of strokes, was somewhat hollow. The Indians, to a man, believed he was caught off bat and pad from Durani when he was only one [...]'[132]

Durani did indeed lose his place in the side for the fourth and fifth Tests. He had only three wickets from his three Tests though of course two of those were vital. But he also failed with the bat with the fractured finger troubling him throughout.

---

[130]Wadekar, Ajit, *My Cricketing Years*, Vikas Publishing House Pvt. Ltd, Delhi, 1973, p. 74.

[131]Gavaskar, Sunil, *Sunny Days*, Rupa Publications, New Delhi, 1976, p. 74.

[132]Cozier, Tony, 'Third Test: Match Drawn', *The Cricketer*, May 1971.

A measly 24 runs from four innings was just not good enough for an all-rounder.

Both the fourth Test at Bridgetown, Barbados, and the fifth and final at Port of Spain, Trinidad, ended in draws. India were victors by a 1–0 margin. In the process, they discovered a legendary talent in opener Gavaskar whose monumental 774 runs in four Tests included a century and double century in the fifth, only the second to do so at the time after Australia's Doug Walters. It remains the highest series aggregate for a debutant and he was splendidly supported by the veteran Sardesai with 642 runs. Together they accounted for all seven centuries scored by India in the series.

Sunder Rajan wrote about Durani in his book, 'An errant genius, Salim Durani can perform miracles one moment and fail abysmally the next. His bowling was one of the highlights of the 1962 tour of West Indies. This time he got a vital breakthrough for India by removing Lloyd and Sobers in quick succession in the second innings of the second Test. He thus played a very significant role in the only Test victory, yet he did little of note in most other matches. Durani hit the first century of the tour against Jamaica, but the move to try him at number three ended up in failure.'[133]

The victory was received with euphoria back home and the players were accorded heroes' welcomes wherever they went. Cricket fever had well and truly gripped the nation. But there was a sterner test ahead—a three-Test series in England where India had never won a Test match in 39 years. Durani was naturally dejected at being dropped for the tour, the third time following 1959 and 1967 he had failed to make the team to England. One of the replacements for England was leg spinner

---

[133] Rajan, Sunder, *India vs West Indies* 1971, Jaico Publishing House, Bombay, 1971, p. 115.

B.S. Chandrasekhar who had been surprisingly omitted for the West Indies series. And what happened in the third and final Test at the Oval meant 1971 went down as the greatest year in the history of Indian cricket. Wadekar and his merry men, it seemed, could do no wrong.

While the team was on tour in the West Indies, Bombay made it 13 in a row by defeating Maharashtra in the 1970–71 Ranji Trophy final. Rajasthan meanwhile fell to Maharashtra in the quarter-finals at Poona—Maharashtra 624 for five declared, Rajasthan 604 all out!

'Durani Trophy'

Barely had the victorious team returned from England when it was time for the start of the 1971–72 domestic season. But not before they received a red carpet welcome at Santa Cruz airport in Bombay and were taken in a triumphant motorcade which crawled its way to Brabourne Stadium as the police struggled to hold back the massive crowd. Everyone wanted a piece of the heroes—whether politicians or ordinary cricket fans. Cricket in India had always enjoyed popularity both at the international and domestic level. But now, unprecedented crowds were packing stadiums everywhere, with Indian cricket basking in the glory of being dubbed unofficial world champions.

England were due to tour India and Pakistan but the tour was postponed due to the political situation. So the full focus was on domestic cricket and there was not an empty seat in the house as the Duleep Trophy kicked off in Nagpur with the fancied North taking on Central Zone in the quarter-final. It was the first step in a dream sequence starring Salim Durani and his unheralded outfit.

Remember, in the previous 10 years of the competition, only West and South Zone had won the title and Central last reached the final in 1965–66. They had also finished runners-up in 1964–65, both times losing by an innings. Durani had turned in brilliant all-round performances in both finals, though in vain. West had emerged champions on five occasions, South on four, and the title was shared between them once.

North were led by Vinay Lamba and had a young team who were confident of putting it across the old guard of Central full of the big names from Rajasthan, as always. But they were in for a shock, swept aside by an innings and 17 runs. North were shot out for a measly 85 on the first day, the lowest total in the competition. The wickets were shared by teenage leg spinner Rakesh Tandon (six for 34) and the wily veteran Durani (four for 20), who was coming off a tremendous stint of bowling for Rajasthan in the Ranji Trophy league stage. Captain Hanumant's 117 not out was well supported by the rest of the batsmen and the declaration came on the second day at 377 for six. North's 275 in the second innings fell far short and it was now Central versus the holders South Zone in the semi-final at Hyderabad, with West having already made it to the final.

South was packed with big names and as the holders, were hot favourites. Led by Venkat, they had eight Test players and one future one in their ranks. It would have been all 11 but Prasanna had ruled himself out by not playing any domestic cricket in the season till that point and Syed Abid Ali dropped out on the eve of the match for personal reasons. 'They Were Embarrassed' was the headline in *Sportsweek* dated 12 March 1972. Indeed they were, embarrassed and humiliated, and once again it was Durani who did the star turn. 'South Zone players strutted like hens as they came to the nets on the pre-match days and on the first day,'[134] read the report. After all, they had in their ranks batting masters like Jaisimha, Vishwanath and

---

[134]'They Were Embarrassed', *Sportsweek*, 12 March 1972.

Pataudi, and future Test player Brijesh Patel. Even without Prasanna, the bowling attack was led by captain Venkat and Chandra. Formidable indeed!

The South Zone selection committee had turned up in force at the Lal Bahadur Shastri stadium to watch their team in action prior to the final against West Zone—a final that was not to be! Even the BCCI had been caught napping. Certain Central would fall to South, they had fixed the dates of the Ranji Trophy pre-quarter final between Madhya Pradesh (who had topped the Central Zone league) against Punjab on the same dates of the Duleep Trophy final. That had to be hurriedly changed.

There were thus plenty of red faces all round as Central pulled off a stunning upset by five wickets. So frustrated were the South's officials and supporters they even condemned umpires S.K. Ghosh and A.K. Guha, deeming them inexperienced, and were critical of the pitch as well. But there was no hiding the fact that the cocky South were outclassed. Pace bowler Kailash Gattani removed openers Abbas Ali Baig and K. Jayantilal with only 10 runs on the board and then Durani got to work with his mesmerizing spin bowling.

Jaisimha (56), Vishwanath (43) and Pataudi (90) were all at their elegant best. The former India captain played a restrained knock on a pitch that offered assistance to the bowlers and looked well set for his century, before he was bowled by a beauty of a leg break by the left-arm magician. It pitched on the leg stump and defeating the defensive prod knocked back the off. Only Prince Salim could have taken out the ex-Nawab with such a gem of a delivery.

South were all out on the first day for 277; Durani had the prize scalps of Jaisimha, Vishwanath and Patel (33) apart from bagging his 'Tiger'. With the pitch his ally, Durani expertly varied his flight and length to finish with the splendid figures of 27.4-6-65-6. Such was the mastery of the conditions that he even out-bowled South's Venkat and Chandra who were fresh from their triumphs in England.

But he was not done yet. He was joint top-scorer with the young Parthasarthi Sharma, both with 83 as they mastered the South spinners and took Central to 309. Durani's innings contained 10 boundaries in 132 minutes. Sharma scored 49 in the second innings as Central sealed the deal by five wickets. Sharma was most impressive and would serve Rajasthan and Central for many years. He made his Test debut in the 1974–75 home series against West Indies.

Could Salim & Co. continue their giant-killing run against another star-studded side in West Zone in the final? The first six in the West line-up were all current or future Test players including the formidable trio of Gavaskar, skipper Wadekar and Sardesai. Bangalore's Central College ground was all decked up to welcome home its heroes—who did not make it. But Central and Durani were not done. Having stunned South, now it was time to scalp West. But it came down to the wire.

'It Was Triumph of Team Spirit' was the headline in *Sportsweek* dated 26 March 1972. Indeed it was, for Central did not have a single current Test player in its ranks. 'The Durani Trophy' was the headline in *The Times of India* (26 March 1972) as the doyen of Indian cricket journalists K.N. Prabhu waxed eloquent about Durani's feats in the tournament. Of course, the 'moody genius' tag was trotted out but after all these years Durani must have gotten used to it.

Wadekar took first strike after winning the toss—a decision he might have regretted later. The dusty pitch took spin from the very start and that was all the help Durani needed. Three wickets fell in the space of four overs before lunch, with Durani capturing the prize scalps of Gavaskar (30) and Wadekar (6) as West limped into the break at 70 for four. The cream of their batting including Sardesai (7) had been sent packing. Hemant Kanitkar, Solkar and Milind Rege took West to 270 for nine by close of the first day. It could have been much worse but for Central's sloppy fielding and wicket-keeping. Durani's opening-day figures were sensational—36-15-40-5. He took his sixth wicket the next morning as West scraped to 279 all out.

But Central's batsmen fared even poorer. Solkar's left-arm spin matched Durani's as he claimed six for 59 with Central all out for 200. Central struck back by stumps on the second day with the wickets of West openers Ramnath Parkar and Gavaskar to keep the match on a knife's edge. Durani picked up three more wickets in the second innings to take his tally in three matches to a record 22 wickets, erasing the previous record of 17 by Baloo Gupte of West in the 1962–63 edition.

West were skittled out for 195, setting Central 275 runs for their maiden title. At 73 for three, it looked like curtains for Central till the reliable pair of Sharma and Durani came together in a match-turning partnership, just as they had done in the semi-final. Sharma's 75 and Durani's 83 not out hauled Central to victory by two wickets, 45 minutes before tea on the fourth and final day. Sharma's fall at 178 for five meant it was all down to the veteran left-hander now and he held firm. His knock had three sixes and five fours as he paced himself perfectly in the nerve-wracking run chase.

When the gallant Gattani joined Durani at 233 for eight, the pendulum had swung back West's way with only Tandon left in the pavilion. Gattani walked to the crease with instructions from captain Hanumant to Durani not to loft the ball even as off spinner Rege was tossing it up to tempt him. But could he be restrained for long? Certainly not! With 10 to win, someone in the press tent shouted that a six and a four would mean victory. Durani could not resist the challenge. He lofted Bombay's master left-arm spinner Padmakar Shivalkar to the mid-wicket boundary with the ball deflecting off the desperate Nicky Saldanha's hand (substituting for Sardesai) for six even as everyone at the ground gasped at the audacity of the shot. It was left to his partner to hit the winning boundary off Rege. The neutral crowd were by now cheering every run as they supported the underdogs. They had long gotten over their disappointment at not seeing their local heroes in action, won over by Durani's captivating batting. They invaded the field but their hero beat them to the safety of the pavilion even as they chanted his name. And all the while the winning team was celebrating the daring victory with gusto as they mobbed the Man of the Tournament.

Gattani remembers the pulsating climax like it was yesterday, 'I reassured Salim when I came in at the fall of the eight wicket that they would not be able to get me out. I blocked one end while he went for the runs at the other. He hugged me after I hit the winning runs and I had tears of joy in my eyes. It was a great feeling—I will never forget that match.'[135] Gattani, who had a first-class century to his credit, hung on grimly for 11 runs.

Cricket fan Vincent Sunder was a 13-year-old when he witnessed the third and penultimate day (13 March 1972). After being set the target of 275, Central were 68 for three at stumps. Earlier in the day, resuming their second innings at 24 for two, West were all out for 195. So there was plenty of action with 11 wickets falling on the day. But his abiding memory is the 'quicksilver run out' by Solkar at forward short leg of opener Suryaveer Singh. It was a dazzling piece of fielding with the batsman stepping out of his crease to play just a defensive push and Solkar throwing down the stumps in one motion. And what of Durani who took three wickets in 26 overs in West's second innings? 'The girls'/women's stand gave him a standing ovation

---

[135]Conversation with the author on 3 September 2023.

every time he got the ball,' Vincent recalled. 'To us wide-eyed little boys it was pure cricket.'[136]

The match was virtually a Bombay versus Rajasthan contest, with 10 from the Ranji champs in the West squad and six from the perennial Ranji Trophy bridesmaids Rajasthan in Central. Durani, in the three matches, scored 237 from five innings (once not out) for an average of 59.25, to go with his rich haul of 22 wickets conceding 230 runs at the incredibly low average of 10.45 and strike rate of 33.81. Durani always described himself as a bowling all-rounder as he gave precedence to his bowling over his batting. But here it was impossible to differentiate between the two—such was his utter dominance with both bat and ball.

What was clear was that at 37 years of age he still had it in him to produce magic and put himself back in contention for a place in the Indian team. It was indeed the Durani Trophy for this splendid all-round show in the tournament that has not been equaled or excelled till this day even after more than 50 years.

Rajasthan, on the other hand, had a disappointing Ranji Trophy season despite their star's sterling bowling with 23 wickets in three matches. They were pushed to second place in the Central Zone league by Madhya Pradesh and were soundly defeated by Mysore in the quarter-final in spite of Durani's nine wickets.

With 69 wickets at 15.04 in 11 first-class matches (five times five or more wickets in an innings, best of six for 44, SR 38.14), Durani was the second highest wicket-taker in the 1971–72 season, just three behind India's vice captain, S. Venkataraghavan of Tamil Nadu.

---

[136]Text message to the author on 6 August 2023.

Last Bow

The new season kicked off in September 1972 with a match to commemorate the hundredth birth anniversary of Ranji in his hometown of Jamnagar. Though the organizers called it a festival match, it was granted first-class status enabling Durani's century (74 and 109 not out) and nine wickets in the match to enter the record books. It was a nostalgic visit back to the town where he had grown up and learned his cricket and he gave the large crowd plenty to cheer. In the same match he passed the landmark of 7,000 career runs and 400 wickets.

The announcement from Lord's in August of the English tour party for the five Tests in India that winter elicited howls of protest from both cricket fans and cricket officials. Once again, the tradition of top names making themselves unavailable for tours to the subcontinent came under a harsh spotlight as captain Ray Illingworth (who had just led England to a 2–2 draw with Australia at home), fast bowler John Snow and opening batsmen John Edrich and Geoff Boycott all decided to take a break.

To rub salt in the wounds, the captain was a debutant! Glamorgan's Tony Lewis had never played a Test match just as was the case with Nigel Howard who captained England to India in 1951–52. None of the 16 had played a Test in India, and four, including Lewis, were without Test experience. Among the big names were left-arm spinner Derek Underwood, wicketkeeper Alan Knott and all-rounder Tony Greig.

With India enthroned as 'unofficial world champions', most of the pundits predicted a cakewalk against this callow side. It did not quite work out that way however. Lewis led the team astutely and batted well. In the end, though India made it a hat-trick of series victories continuing on from the golden year of 1971, the 2–1 verdict could so easily have gone the other way.

The shock came right at the start. England won the first Test at New Delhi by six wickets, with Lewis leading the way with a match-winning 70 not out on 25 December to make it a Christmas to remember for the jubilant tourists. Naturally, a sense of shock and dismay swept the country. It had been eight Test matches without defeat for India and now they had been outplayed by a bunch of rookies led by a captain on Test debut, no less!

'A Betrayal by Indian Batsmen', screamed the headline in *Sportsweek* (31 December 1972) as former Test opener Mushtaq Ali condemned them for miserable totals of 173 and 233. Naturally, changes had to be made and out went two of the star performers of 1971, Venkat and Sardesai, for the second Test at Calcutta. They were replaced by Prasanna and Durani.

Durani was an obvious choice. Hardly had the team for the Delhi Test been announced when he practically kicked down the door of the selectors as he starred for Central Zone in their drawn match against the tourists at Indore. Though opener Suryaveer Singh had the distinction of being the first to register a century against them, it was Durani who stood out with a brilliant display of power hitting, particularly against off spinner Pat Pocock, racing to his 50 in 68 minutes with 11 boundaries. When skipper Hanumant declared at 255 for three, six runs behind England, he was not out on 81 with 16 boundaries.

Of course, Durani being Durani, he was not done yet. He tied down the English batsmen in their second innings, taking all three wickets to fall to the bowlers, one being run out as the declaration came late on the final day, his figures reading 31-11-66-3. Wadekar had joked after the Delhi Test that India had presented Lewis and his men a Christmas gift and now it was Lewis' turn to give the Indians a New Year's gift. And that is exactly what happened at Calcutta, though, till the very end, the result was in doubt.

The series has been immortalized in the first full-length cricket documentary in India directed and presented by the cricket and film journalist Raju Bharatan. *The Victory Story* was produced by the National Films Division and released in 1974, and over 112 minutes it is a vivid record of a series that produced thrilling cricket even if the batting of both sides did not match up to the quality of the bowling.

Having been starved of international cricket for three years, the fervor throughout the tour was at an all-time high with every ground packed to capacity even outside the five Tests. Eden Gardens, with its massive stadium, of course topped the bill and lakhs of fans—over five days—spilled onto the ground to celebrate after India won by 28 runs to square the series.

While watching the documentary, my focus was naturally on Durani's batting. He did take one wicket in his three Tests, that of Greig in the third Test at Madras, to finish his Test career with 75 wickets. But he was overshadowed by the brilliance of our famous spin quartet who took 71 of the 75 English wickets to fall to the bowlers in the series.

Durani played a lead role in both the victories at Calcutta and in the third Test at Madras, which India won by four wickets to take a 2–1 lead in the series, a lead they held on to. The fourth Test at Kanpur and the fifth at Bombay both ended in draws as the batsmen finally came into their own towards the fag end of the series. With the bowlers holding sway at Calcutta, there were only three half-centuries on both sides, two for India (Engineer and Durani) and one by Greig for England. So Durani's 53 in the paltry second innings of 155 was invaluable.

What was pathetic to watch was his limping between the wickets. In the second innings, he was allowed a runner in Gavaskar. Durani said he had gone to a party with Engineer on the rest day which fell between the third and fourth days of the

Test and slipped in the washroom, pulling his right hamstring.[137]

Batting virtually on one leg, Durani smote seven boundaries and a six off Underwood. His partnership worth 71 for the third wicket with Vishwanath was the highest for India and swung the match in their favour. England's opening bowler Geoff Arnold told him sarcastically, 'You are the prince of Indian cricket. You don't field or bowl and when you bat you have a runner.'[138]

That six off Underwood came right after his fervent fans in the then-Ranji Stand were chanting for a big hit from their hero. He promptly hoisted England's star bowler over mid-wicket and into the top tier of the stand to send the spectators into a frenzy of excitement. Durani, in an article in 1978, picked this innings of 53 as his best since he was struggling with the injury and because it swung the Test India's way. He credits his runner Gavaskar with a piece of advice that made all the difference.

'I was in a state of mind that could only be called miserable as the injury was hampering me. The English bowlers were making me stretch outside the off stump. I found this a painful process and was groping most of the time [...] Gavaskar told me not to reach for the ball outside the off stump but instead to shuffle back on the middle stump and then go forward. Like a magic formula, this method began paying dividends and I began to open out with strokes of controlled aggression [...] I value this innings for the fine piece of team-spirit which made the big difference to the fortunes of the side.'[139]

He carried the injury over to the Madras Test and now there were murmurings of protest from the English camp. That injury was exacerbated when he pulled a groin muscle on the

---

[137] 'Gollapudi, Nagraj, 'The Salim and Giffy Show', *Cricinfo Magazine*, January 2006.
[138] Munwani, Haresh, 'My Cricketing Years', *Sportsworld*, 1 November 1978.
[139] Durani, Salim, 'My Best Innings…Tip that paid off', *Cricket Quarterly*, July-September 1978.

third day. Ever the diplomat, Lewis decided not to make an issue of it, something an Illingworth or Bill Lawry would surely have done. The point of contention was whether he was injured during the match to deserve a runner. He had no choice but to field though, and was a terrible liability due to his lack of mobility. In Calcutta, he dropped Dennis Amiss and at Madras let off Lewis. He was, once again, allowed a runner in the first innings at Madras but not in the second when his hobbling meant that twos were reduced to singles.

This time though, the showman was overshadowed by the dramatic comeback into the team by Pataudi, who outscored his old rival with a delightful 73 on his return. Durani laboured to 38 from 161 balls in the first innings, one of the slowest innings of his career, and for once the crowd booed him as he was stuck for 40 minutes without scoring. He reacted by swinging left-arm spinner Norman Gifford over mid-wicket for six before he limped off as Gifford had him caught and bowled. The two were having a running battle on the tour starting with the match against Central Zone at Indore before the start of the Test series, where in the battle of lefties it was the batsman who took a heavy toll of the bowler.

For the first time in the series, a total of 300 was crossed and India's 316 meant they had a lead of 74 runs. England's second innings crumbled to 159 with Durani somehow getting through 15 overs to bag the vital wicket of Greig. And now the victory target was a mere 86.

But as wicket after wicket tumbled, that tiny target assumed daunting proportions. Durani, though, was unflustered. He repeated his first innings score of 38, but this time he was back in his natural elements despite his physical discomfort.

In the first innings, he had Chetan Chauhan as his runner, the second time around he was on his own. Gifford had a confident appeal for lbw turned down and had words with his rival, who promptly went on to clout him over the boundary. He had another six and three fours till he was lbw to Pocock for 38 off 77 balls at 67 for eight. More than half the runs had come off his bat at that stage and India finally scrambled home by four wickets after the umpire signaled a no-ball. Once again, his innings proved a match-winning one as it had in the previous Test at Calcutta.

Fan Frenzy

The selectors were now pushed into a corner by his fitness issues and had no choice but to drop him for the fourth Test at Kanpur, which ended in a tame draw. Durani claimed to be fit but he failed a medical test conducted by the BCCI. His countless fans were having nothing of it though. They launched a campaign to have their hero reinstated for the fifth and final Test, at Bombay. Newspaper and magazine offices were deluged by letters claiming the medical test was a hoax, with cables even being sent to the Prime Minister's Office!

Things got out of hand when posters demanding his return started appearing around Bombay on the eve of the final Test. 'No Durani, No Test Here', 'Selectors Don't Be Stupid Like Vijay Merchant', read another—these were published in *Sportsweek* (4 February 1973), which carried an editorial, 'Stop This Poster Campaign', condemning it as blackmail.

In the event, the veteran was passed fit. But was he really? The limping continued in Bombay, as did the run scoring and six hitting, though he did not demand a runner this time. There were two sixes in his first innings (73), the first off Underwood into his favourite East Stand just as his fans were chanting for one and the second off Jack Birkenshaw which took him from 49 to 55. The roar from the stands echoed all across the stadium.

Durani was still in pain and an attempted sweep on one knee saw him grimace in pain—this I spotted in the documentary. The crowd was willing him onto a century which would have seen him joining Engineer and Vishwanath in this Test. But Pocock got him in the first innings and in the second too. That second innings of 37 included another six which made it seven in his three Tests in the series—more than all his teammates put together could muster. The campaign by his supporters had placed a huge burden on Durani, as he explained in an interview in 1983. 'I alone know how tense I was. I had never been worried earlier, but now it was different, for the support of the people had been overwhelming. By the grace of God I did well [...] But I still shudder to think of what would have happened had I failed.'[140]

Gattani remembered with a chuckle how he would treat left-arm spinners with contempt, 'Whether it be Bedi, Shivalkar, Gifford or Underwood, *unke patloon nikalte the* [he would take their pants off]. He targeted them as he considered them competitors to his own left arm-spin.'[141]

For Durani it was a bittersweet series. Wrote Sunder Rajan in his summing-up, 'Durani was clearly a liability in the field and a positive embarrassment all round. Yet his batting was superb. That he could treat almost all the bowlers with contempt despite his physical handicap spoke volumes for his abilities. The best way for the Board to handle an errant genius like Durani is to tell him firmly that his selection would depend entirely on his physical fitness. England were determined not to allow him a runner or substitute in the fifth Test. Durani perhaps sensed the mood and never asked for one.'[142]

---

[140]Memon, Ayaz, 'Mr Sixer!,' *Cricketer Asia*, July 1983.
[141]Conversation with the author, 3 September 2023.
[142]*The Hat-Trick: MCC Tour of India—72-73*, Sunder Rajan (ed.), Jaico Books, Bombay, 1974, p. 118.

Engineer topped the batting averages with 41.50, followed by Vishwanath on 40.55, and just a fraction behind was Durani on 40.50. In a generally low-scoring series, his batting had made all the difference. Neither Durani nor anyone else for that matter would have known at the time that this happened to be his twenty-ninth and final Test. The next series for India was in any case nearly 18 months away in mid-1974.

Back in January 1960, at the same Brabourne stadium, the journey had begun and now 13 years later it had ended with a total of 110 runs in his last two innings. India won six of his 29 Tests and lost seven with 16 draws. In each of those six victories, Durani played a role proving that at his best he was a match-winner. But in that period India played 65 Tests, meaning he missed more matches than he played in. Of the 36 he missed, India won seven (including five versus New Zealand, the weakest team at the time), lost 15 and drew 14. No wonder, then, that Dilip Doshi called him a 'wasted genius' that Indian cricket failed to utilize to the maximum.

England's off spinner, Pat Pocock, took 14 wickets in four Tests on the tour including Durani in both innings at Bombay. I approached Pocock for his memories of the series 50 years before and this was his reply by mail, 'I did not know Salim that well but he certainly had some amazing features! Tall, good looking man, who looked as though he had come straight out of Bollywood. Being so tall he had long levers on the cricket field and was a natural striker of the ball and a slightly 'slingy' action when he bowled his spinners, totally different to Bishan Bedi. He scored plenty of runs in the Test matches but there is one aspect about him I will never forget. On a few occasions the crowd shouted and chanted, "We want a sixer, we want a sixer", and many times he obliged by striking a big six! When I bowled to him if I gave the ball any air I had to expect it to be hit for six. He was however not a great fielder, very slow mover. On one occasion he ran around the boundary to cut off a ball and put his foot out to stop the ball—the ball hopped over his foot and went for four runs. Long may Salim's memory live on!'[143]

The 'six on demand' myth lingered on even after his death, even as Durani sought to laugh it off during his lifetime. In an article in 1984 he explained his philosophy and style. 'People used to say I hit sixers on demand be it a Ranji or Duleep Trophy match or be it a Test match. Looking back however I feel these sixers that delighted the public were divine coincidences. It is not possible to hit a sixer on demand. Nevertheless, I am supremely grateful to my fans who gave me the appellation of "MR SIXER" [...] Come to think of it, hitting a sixer is not all that difficult. Timing and the added touch of wrists are important.'[144]

If the Test series had been a bittersweet experience for Durani, the domestic season had been more bitter than sweet. For the first time, Vidarbha defeated Rajasthan in the Central Zone league opening tie and after conceding the first innings lead in the next against Madhya Pradesh, Rajasthan's third and final match in the zone against Uttar Pradesh was a must-win. They came agonizingly close after Uttar Pradesh followed on. But they clung on for a draw with their last wicket pair at the crease. A precious 20 minutes was wasted at the start of the match as the matting was not properly laid at the new Sawai Man Singh stadium. That proved crucial for the hosts and they had the humiliation of finishing third out of the four teams in the league, thus missing out on a knockout berth.

For Durani, it was a crushing blow as he scored 114 and took four wickets in the first innings. The century proved to be his fourteenth and final in first-class cricket, half of which

---

[143]Email to the author, 5 August 2023.
[144]Durani, Salim, 'So...You Want a SIXER!', *Indian Cricketer*, December 1984.

came while representing Rajasthan in the Ranji Trophy. It was cold comfort that Central Zone made the final of the Duleep Trophy for the second season in succession, though this time they were trounced by West by an innings.

Shocker at Delhi

The 1973–74 domestic season assumed major proportions as players around the country were desperate to impress the selectors and gain a berth in the team to England which would be announced at the end of the season in March 1974.

Once again Rajasthan's final match in the league phase was a must-win. And this they did against Madhya Pradesh to top the zone. But it was close and came about with a daring declaration in the second innings at 70 for five, setting Madhya Pradesh a target of 214 and then match-winning bowling by Durani. That they collapsed for 148 was due to him alone. Just past his thirty-ninth birthday, there was still magic in those fingers. Three wickets in the first innings, seven for 46 in the second (his second best bowling figures) for a match haul of 10 for 84, the best of his career. Could his dream of finally making a Test tour of England on his fourth attempt now come to fruition?

The dream sadly turned to dust on the dusty pitch of the Karnail Singh Stadium down the road from the New Delhi Railway station when Rajasthan faced Railways in the quarter-final in March 1974.

The man who had given him his first break in Test cricket in January 1960 as chairman of the selectors, Lala Amarnath was living in the Railway Officers' quarters in the neighbouring Panchkuian Road barely half a kilometre away and specially came to watch Durani in action. So did the rest of the spectators in the sparse concrete stands in one of the Capital's half-dozen first-class venues and one of its most nondescript.

Durani did not disappoint either Amarnath or his fans. But while the stands echoed with the usual cries for a six, Durani put his head down and played a highly responsible innings. His innings lasting 228 minutes and was full of stylish cuts and drives. But when on 96 and with his century just one shot away, he was hit flush on the face by the tall, lanky Railways medium pacer Gunwant Desai bowling with the new ball with Rajasthan's total reading 223 for three.

Sportsweek's reporter on the spot described the delivery as short but innocuous. 'It was a gift for the asking. Durani could have swung the ball over the fence, but he swung his bat too early and was hit flush on the face. He fell in a heap and was rushed to the hospital. Apart from a fractured nose, he needed plastic surgery, too, and the doctors advised him complete rest for three to four weeks.'[145]

So, on the very first day, Durani was done for the match as he was admitted to the Northern Railway hospital across the road from the stadium. Shocked by the injury to their senior player, Rajasthan subsided to 255. It was just about enough as their rivals fell nine runs short on the first innings and Rajasthan were through to the semi-final. Here they squeaked past Hyderabad by 12 runs to face Karnataka in the final. Led by Prasanna, Karnataka had finally ended the reign of 15 successive years of the formidable Bombay in the other semi-final.

The youngest of Lala Amarnath's three sons, Rajender (AKA Johnny) recalled being told of the incident at their home in the evening.

'I was not at the match but when I heard Salim bhai had been admitted to hospital I visited him in the evening. He was in a jovial mood as usual and joked that it was a pity such a good looking guy had been hit on his face! Sitting by the bedside was

---

[145] *Sportsweek*, 17 March 1974.

a pretty young lady who I did not recognize. He introduced me to her—it was the actress Parveen Babi who had flown down from Bombay to be at this bedside. After he was discharged he visited our home. Dad had given him his first break in Test cricket back in 1960 and he always called him papa-*ji* and my mother mummy-*ji*.'[146] This was just a year after the release of the movie *Charitra* starring Babi and Durani.

From the 1960–61 season to 1973–74—14 seasons in all—Rajasthan had now made it to the final on eight occasions. But this was their first final since 1969–70. Each time they faced the heartbreak of finishing on the losing side to Bombay. Finally, they had a different opponent. Karnataka were formidable rivals, full of current and future Test players, including the magnificent trio of Vishwanath, Prasanna and Chandrasekhar.

For Rajasthan's skipper Hanumant Singh, this felt like his final shot at glory. Desperate for the services of his star player, he pleaded with Durani to leave his hospital bed in Delhi even if he was not fully fit. This was the third time Jaipur was hosting the final but the first at the Sawai Mansingh Stadium. For Karnataka, it was their second shot at glory having lost to Bombay in the 1941–42 season when still known as Mysore.

According to Rajan Bala reporting the final for *Sportsweek*, the pitch was ideal for left arm-spinners and Durani bowled a splendid spell in the first innings with three for 70 (and two for 58 in the second innings) including the wickets of Vishwanath and Patel, who was being touted as the new batting sensation of Indian cricket. Bala wrote that the veteran bowler made the rookie batsman look like a novice.

Sadly, Durani got his first and only 'pair' (duck in both innings) in domestic cricket and Karnataka achieved their dream of their maiden national title, while the nightmare continued

---

[146]Conversation with the author on 17 September 2023.

for Rajasthan. Bala was convinced that Durani's injury was more serious than what was believed at the time and felt if he had been fitter ('and younger') he would have routed the Karnataka batting in both innings on such a helpful pitch.

Earlier in the season Durani had his first taste of limited-overs cricket. The BCCI had introduced the 60-overs Deodhar Trophy with an eye to the inaugural Prudential World Cup slated for 1975 in England. In the defeat to South Zone in the semi-final, he had the excellent bowling figures of 12-4-23-2 for Central Zone with the wickets of Jayantilal and Vishwanath and scored 21. He played just three List A (domestic limited-overs) games in his entire career but for the rest of his life had to answer the question of whether he would have relished limited-overs cricket including T20s. The answer is obvious—it would have suited his game to a 'T'.

The terrible injury put paid to his hopes of making it to England on the 1974 tour and his desire to play at least one Test at Lord's. Though he played on intermittently till 1977–78, he managed only 13 matches in the four seasons following the injury. He continued to bowl with some success but his batting suffered, with just one half-century in those 13 matches.

In a chance meeting in September 2008 with S. Giridhar, co-author of the book *Mid-Wicket Tales*, at the Delhi airport lounge, he recounted the injury when discussing how tail-end batsmen in his days avoided getting hit when helmets were not in vogue.

'He pauses, looks up at the roof, almost in contemplation and then says, but don't think people did not get hurt [in pre-helmet days]. I finished with cricket in 1974 after being felled by a bouncer in a Ranji match. I was batting on 94 [actually 96] when a bouncer from Gunwant Desai struck me down. They had to operate on me. And he parts his black hair (dyed or natural?) to show me where the surgeon had to do his stuff.'[147]

There was one last chance to force his way back into the national team when West Indies toured India in 1974–75. Their tour match against Central Zone at Nagpur was his final realistic bid. Cruel luck, then, that a controversial decision should go against him in the first innings just as he was getting nicely into his stride.

He cut and straight drove off spinner Albert Padmore, and then on drove him to the boundary. Padmore got his wicket when Durani attempted to drive and missed and the next thing he knew the bails had fallen. He stood rooted to his crease as he was certain the ball had rebounded off wicketkeeper David Murray's pads and hit the stumps. It took umpire J.D. Ghosh more than a minute to deliberate before giving him out. Durani looked baffled when the umpire raised his finger as the fielders persisted with their appeal and trudged back dejected to the pavilion. With four boundaries in his 23, he had put on 58 runs in only 34 minutes for the third wicket with centurion Murthy Rajan.

The decision rankled him for the rest of his life. His two wickets, Alvin Kallicharan and Murray, came at a heavy cost. His chance had slipped away.

Sunder Rajan wrote, 'Much interest centred round how well Salim Durani would fare. The old warhorse still had some class and his come-back against England at home in 1972–73 was green in memory. There was a question mark about his fitness, though, but his fans, who are legion were hoping and praying he would be able to prove his fitness and form against the West Indians. Had he lived up to expectations there can be no doubt that Durani would have staged another remarkable come-back for there were still many gaps in India's batting order. Durani was not unaware

---

[147]Giridhar, S., and V.J. Raghunath, *Mid-Wicket Tales: From Trumper to Tendulkar*, Sage Publications, New Delhi, 2020, p. 89.

of his chance. In fact, he seemed determined to make good.'[148]

He rued the decision in an interview in 1983, 'I did have a chance of getting back when I played well for Central Zone against West Indies in 1974–75. I was given out to a doubtful decision. A bigger innings then would probably have seen me back in the side.'[149] The match was staged between the second Test at New Delhi and the third at Calcutta. India had lost both the first at Bangalore and then at Delhi and were facing a batting crisis, so there was scope for his return. Sadly, that chance slipped away.

There was one last match against a touring side, his twelfth since his first against the New Zealanders way back in December 1955. This was against England for Central Zone at Jaipur in December 1976. It would be his final appearance at his home ground, but it was no grand farewell. He took a cross-batted swipe at left-arm pace bowler John Lever and was bowled for nine; second innings run out for one. He took just one wicket, that of century-maker Graham Barlow in the first innings. It was clear by now that post the injury his batting was relying more on memory and instinct rather than on technique and timing.

The final bow came in the 1977–78 season. But even at 43, right till the end, he was chipping in with useful bowling performances. In the Ranji pre-quarter finals against Maharashtra, he picked up six wickets in the match as Rajasthan won by four wickets.

Feroze Shah Kotla in New Delhi would prove to be the stage for his final match on the national stage. Rajasthan were up against last season's runners-up Delhi led by Test captain Bishan Bedi. There were eight current or former players in their

---

[148]Rajan, Sunder, *India vs West Indies 1974–75*, Jaico Publishing House, Bombay, 1975, p. 63.
[149]Memon, Ayaz, 'Mr Sixer', *Cricketer Asia*, July 1983.

side as against just three for Rajasthan, who were outgunned from the start and crushed by an innings and 110 runs. Durani bowled a marathon 44 overs in Delhi's huge total of 552 for nine declared and picked up the wicket of future Test opening batsman Arun Lal for 117.

Out for a duck in the first innings, the showman was not done yet as Rajasthan followed on. On his last day in first-class cricket, Durani had one final point to make and it was against the cocky youngster who had scored that century. Arun Lal was aged just 22—Durani almost double that at 43—and made the rookie mistake of pricking the veteran's pride. He responded as only he could—yes, like a genius. And it was a lesson surely well learned by Lal who would go on to play 16 Test matches.

It was 1 March 1978 and Durani was determined to go out not with a whimper but with a bang. The result was a delightful cameo innings of 44.

Lal said, 'Durani bowled down the leg and turned one sharply to hit my off-stump bail. Being young and excitable I was quite peeved [...] Durani came out to bat. Rakesh Shukla was bowling, I was at slip and started ribbing him [...] [he] just looked at me.

'Then the fun started but not for Lal—the next four balls Durani sliced to third man just subtly enough to force the fielder to chase each one to the boundary, but in vain. The third delivery in fact was pitched just outside leg stump "but believe it or not, he withdrew outside the line and sliced it once more [...] I [was] puffing and panting [...] he said, *"Hum ko bhi thoda cricket aata hain."* ["Even I know how to play a little cricket."] He was a genius.'[150]

Touché!

---

[150]Bhattacharya, Rahul, 'A touch of Durani', *Wisden Asia Cricket*, September 2002.

Six

Life after Cricket

He played his final competitive first-class match at the Kotla in 1978. However, that was not the last time Salim Durani was known to have stepped onto a cricket field. It was at the unlikely Al Maktoum stadium in Dubai on 5 and 6 March 1981 that Durani was part of an unusual India and Pakistani XI, which had in its ranks Bishan Singh Bedi, Imran Khan, Mohinder Amarnath, Wasim Raja and others, taking on an England XI in two matches for the benefit of Pakistan's batsman Younis Ahmed.

Their opponents were an England XI including Pat Pocock, Alan Butcher, John Lever, Keith Fletcher and our very own Farokh Engineer, by dint of having represented the English county of Lancashire from 1968 to 1976. Of course, these were unofficial exhibition games played in a festive spirit in which Durani at the age of 46 scored 23 and 32. But one of the lesser-known participants remembers a different side to the game.

Delhi left-arm pace bowler Sunil Valson was still two years away from being a member of the Prudential World Cup-winning squad and was Durani's roommate in Dubai. 'They were fun games so we were all surprised that Imran was bowling full tilt,' Valson told me with a chuckle. Durani was twice Valson's age but they hit it off in those few days together in the Dubai desert. 'We all called him "uncle". He was fun-loving and great company. Whenever Delhi or North Zone came to Mumbai for matches he would come to meet us. He was loved by each and everyone.'[151]

The Big-Screen Stint

Like so many cricketers before and since, Durani too was taken in by the glamour of the Hindi film world. He was great friends with Dev Anand and fellow-Pathan Dilip Kumar (real name Mohammed Yusuf Khan), as well as many other superstars of his era. Given his dashing good looks, it was only natural that he would be the first Indian cricketer to have a major role in a movie.

'The nawabs of Hyderabad notwithstanding, Durani was surely the handsomest Indian to play big cricket, and he even acted, purely on the basis of his looks, in a Hindi feature film,' wrote Ramachandra Guha.[152]

The movie was *Charitra*, which released in the same year as his final Test match and starred the teenage Parveen Babi in the first movie of a storied career that would see her on the cover of *Time* magazine in 1976 as the face of Indian cinema. But before *Charitra*, he also had a role in *Aakhri Din Pehli Raat*, directed by Kamal Amrohi, the husband of the legendary Meena Kumari, who reportedly wrote the script. Unfortunately, due to budgetary reasons the movie was never completed or released. It depicted him as a playboy to whom pretty women were easily attracted. It was announced in 1966 that he had signed a two-year two-picture deal and the second one was likely to feature him as a cricketer. It was made clear that the shooting of the movies would not restrict his cricket career, which was at its peak at the time. But it never did happen until seven years later.

---

[151]Conversation with the author on 9 August 2023.
[152]Guha, Ramachandra, *Wickets in the East: An Anecdotal History*, Oxford University Press, New Delhi, 1991, p. 144.

Charitra was directed by the controversial Babu Ram Ishara, who made a name for himself in the 1970s tackling what was then considered 'bold' themes, like sexuality.

'The tall light-eyed Salim Durani was cast in the role of Ashok, a rich playboy who has a different woman in his bed every night,' wrote film journalist and author Karishma Upadhyay.[153] So what is clear from his very brief fling with filmdom is that he was being typecast as per his image off the field.

I had asked Bishan Bedi for his views on Durani as a bowler. The request was forwarded via his wife Anju since he was then ailing. This is the reply I received, 'When I ask, all he says is "wonderful human being always surrounded by women!"'[154]

Reviews of the movie were poor and it bombed at the box office. It did, however, launch Babi on her career, something that Durani took a little pride in. The fact that she hailed from Junagadh, in then Saurashtra (and had a touch of nobility in her family), meant Parveen and Salim had much in common and got along on the sets. Rumours of her falling head over heels for her much older married co-star are probably typical of pre-movie publicity that used to be conveniently 'leaked' to give the movie a high-profile launch.

In an interview with the late Pradeep Vijayakar, Durani gave an explanation of the plot of *Charitra* and his role in it. 'It's a social suspense drama and takes a hard look at our society and what you see is something to be ashamed of. It has a good story and strong content. And there is a careful exclusion of cheap *masala*.' As for his character in the film, he said, 'I play a sort of dashing role (the film is fairly hot) opposite Parveen Babi. Gautam Sarin has an equally important role.'[155]

---

[153] Upadhyay, Karishma, *Parveen Babi,* Hachette India, New Delhi, 2020, p. 53. With thanks to the author for her inputs for this section.

[154] Text to author dated 2 June 2023. (Bedi passed away four months later.)

[155] Vijayakar, Pradeep, 'Salim Durani: Films Are Okay but Cricket Ambition Stays', *Sportsweek,* 22 July 1973.

Hard Times

In an interview with *Filmfare*, he admitted he still loved playing cricket but it was not paying the bills. 'I have to earn money and I am looking for a job even now,' he said during the shoot in Poona.[156] That was an issue with Durani that dogged him all his life. He was perennially short of employment and funds. Generous to a fault, his hangers-on also took advantage of him.

The Cricketers Benefit Fund Series, set up in Sharjah by Sheikh Abdul Rahman Bukhatir, used to present generous purses to retired cricketers from India and Pakistan during the event's heydays in the 1980s and 90s when matches in the desert kingdom drew huge crowds.

Seeing Durani was hard up, an out-of-turn purse of $35,000 was organized for him in 1984. Durani took 10 of his friends with him to Sharjah and covered all their expenses. He bought expensive electronic goods for them that were then not available in India and were much sought after. But when they returned to Mumbai they had no funds to pay the heavy customs duty and everything was confiscated.

'So, Salim bhai's Sharjah benefit match earnings were spent entirely on his friends! That's the kind of person he was—he never cared for money and once he had money in his pocket, he would spend it all on his loved ones,' was written in a tribute following his passing.[157]

Another example of his large-heartedness is an oft-repeated story concerning the young Sunil Gavaskar with whom he shared a special bond. 'Money is a commodity which Salim will

---

[156]*Filmfare*, 15 June 1973.
[157]Das, Soumitra, 'Salim Durani Would Spend All His Money on His Friends: Anshuman Gaekwad', *The Times of India*, 5 April 2023, http://tinyurl.com/2ht8fxf7. Accessed on 16 February 2024.

never be able to keep. He is so generous and warm-hearted that he will go out of his way to help anybody,' wrote Gavaskar.[158]

It was on an overnight train journey from Guntur to Madras in 1971 before the West Indies tour that they found themselves travelling together after a match. Durani had organized a bed roll for himself but the young Gavaskar was shivering in the cold winter night. Salim gave him a blanket and sheet to cover himself. 'When I woke up the next morning I saw Salim fast asleep, all huddled up to keep himself warm. I couldn't believe it. An established Test cricketer and a hero had given his only blanket and sheet to a young unknown Ranji Trophy player. This overwhelmingly generous and totally unselfish side to Salim's personality is not known to many who only point out his faults. From that day Salim became uncle to me.'[159]

Longtime teammate and dear friend Kailash Gattani, who served Rajasthan and Central Zone loyally for 20 years, also recalls how big-hearted Durani was. 'He had a soft spot for everyone. If a beggar approached he would dip into his pocket and hand over whatever he had, even if it was a twenty-rupee note.'[160]

The BCCI also organized two benefit matches for Durani. Allegedly, he was duped of the funds. In 2011, the BCCI honoured him with their annual C.K. Nayudu Lifetime Achievement Award and a purse of ₹15 lakh. This and his monthly BCCI pension of ₹60,000 saw him through till the end.

In Australian historian Dr Richard Cashman's path-breaking book *Patrons, Players and the Crowd: The Phenomenon of Indian Cricket*, there are details such as height, educational background, occupation(s), father's occupation and so on of all Indian Test

---

[158]Gavaskar, Sunil, *Sunny Days*, Rupa Publications, New Delhi, 1976, p. 238.
[159]Ibid.
[160]Conversation with the author on 3 September 2023.

cricketers till 1980. These nuggets of information cannot be found in any other book on Indian cricket and it is a pity it has never been updated. Durani's occupations are listed as the following: Service of Mewar; Mukund Iron and Steel; J.K. Chemicals and Century Rayon. Not listed is Spencer's of Madras and obviously jobs post-1980.[161]

Ayaz Memon in his interview/feature in the *Illustrated Weekly of India* paints a sad picture of the dire financial state Durani was in at the time. He was living in a rundown dormitory style lodge 'for the working homeless' in a Mumbai suburb where he was squeezed into a cramped room. In American terms it would be called a 'flop house'. The rent was waived by the owners due to his fame as a cricketer. Durani was candid in the interview. 'I missed guidance, nobody advised me. I was not a settled man, hopping around, making my own decisions, getting in and out of trouble.'[162]

This erratic existence took a heavy toll on his personal and professional life. His marriage to Rekha broke up and he then married a doctor from the Jain community from Gujarat. Her tragic death in 1989 left him heartbroken and helpless. In his old age, he sold his ancestral property (Durani House) and moved in with his brother's family in Jamnagar. Looking for another source of income, Durani also tried his hand at commentary in the mid-1980s. It was without success but it did have its lighter moments.

One of the doyens of cricket commentary, Dr Narottam Puri, recalls how the naïve Durani fell for a prank during their TV commentary stint together.

Dr Puri recounted in a book by Fredun De Vitre how

---

[161]Cashman, Richard, *Patrons, Players and the Crowd: The Phenomenon of Indian Cricket*, Orient Longman Limited, New Delhi, 1980, p. 177.
[162]Ayaz Memon, 'Mr. Sixer', *Illustrated Weekly of India*, 23-24 March 1991.

Durani developed a peculiarity, referring to all-rounder Roger Binny as 'Rogers' Binny. This made Durani the butt of jokes on the cricket circuit after he had made his Hindi commentary debut on Doordarshan during the first Test versus the West Indies at Kanpur in 1983–84.

There was a popular soft drink sold in Bombay at the time called Roger's. The speculation back then was this is what confused Durani. When the series reached Bombay for the fourth Test, a humour column appeared in a local daily claiming Binny's wife was planning to sue Durani 'for adding a new fizz to her life', referencing the soft drink brand. The piece even added that his colleagues in the commentary box would be called as witnesses in the court action. Of course, it was all in jest.

'Poor Salim! The moment he read it, he turned pale. To add to his problems, "Tiger" Pataudi, the expert, painted a horrible picture for Salim if he were convicted in such legal proceedings [...]' In desperation, he turned for assistance to fellow commentator De Vitre, a leading lawyer, even while the other commentators were roaring in laughter at his expense.[163]

Dr Puri paid tribute to Durani via email, 'Dashing, debonair, epitome of cricket in those years and for all he did on and off the field, it was but natural for anyone to be attracted to Salim bhai. Like everyone else I was a fan of his grace and his repertoire, both in batting and bowling.

'I met him as an expert commentator on *Doordarshan* and realized what a gentle soul he was. He was quite a draw for autograph hunters and we basked in his glory. He was not the most articulate and expressive but what he opined in a simple, unostentatious way was always worth listening to. He was

---

[163]De Vitre, Fredun, *Willow Tales—The Lighter Side of Indian Cricket*, The Marine Sports Publishing Division, Bombay, 1993, p. 66.

wonderful, no airs about him and was a star even a decade after his glory days were over. He did not do much commentary after this stint but the afterglow that he left on all of his colleagues in the box is still fresh in memory.'[164]

A Prince Till the Very End

Though I had occasionally seen him being plied with drinks by journalist fans in the Press Club of India—his favourite watering hole in the Capital—the last time I spoke to Durani was in October 2007. The Press Club had organized a discussion anchored by Charu Sharma on the future of the new T20 format following India's stunning victory in the inaugural T20 World Cup in South Africa.

As reporters gathered round to speak to him, all the talk centred around how Durani would have been in his elements in the format, which would take the cricket world by storm the very next year with the launch of the IPL. Durani, of course, said he would have loved playing both 50-over and 20-over cricket as it was ideally suited to his style of cricket.

There was an awkward moment when a young reporter asked him his name. We were momentarily stunned but Durani laughed it off, saying, *'Beti*, ask your papa, he will tell you who I am.'

One of those journalists at the Press Club told me he was interviewing Durani for a biography. Sadly, the journalist passed away not long after and the book never appeared. In fact, a book by/on Durani has been a recurring theme since the 1970s. In the 1973 *Sportsweek* interview with Pradeep Vijayakar, he said he planned to call it 'Ask for Six'. 'Don't expect anything ultra-controversial. I'm not so petty as to rake up old

---

[164] Email to the author dated 24 July 2023.

controversies. Of course, some nasty characters are waiting to be exposed. But I'm not certain I'm the one who is going to do it.'[165]

After the two years of isolation and stress brought on by the spread of Covid, Durani's health took a turn for the worse. Sadly, he suffered towards the end after undergoing surgery for a broken thigh bone following a fall at home in January 2023. The end finally came on 2 April. The only cricketer to attend his funeral in Jamnagar was Ajay Jadeja of the erstwhile Ranji royal family who had been benefactors to both Salim and father Abdul. The select few who were allowed to see him towards the end were devastated by the pitiable condition of this once proud and handsome man.

Not since the death of Tiger Pataudi in 2011 had there been such an outpouring of emotion over the passing of an Indian cricketer. Remember, Durani had played his final Test match 50 years ago and in this day and age, when attention spans are measured in nanoseconds and everyone, no matter how undeserving, has their 15 minutes, rather 15 seconds, of fame, it was remarkable to see the media coverage after Durani's death. That, too, in the midst of blanket coverage of the IPL.

The Indian Express Delhi edition of 3 April 2023 had an eight-column banner headline right across the back page proclaiming 'Flamboyant Cricketer, Movie Star, Nice Guy, Ultimate Entertainer.'[166] In the same edition, former all-rounder Karsan Ghavri, Durani's closest friend among cricketers, wrote, 'Hero worship of cricketers began with Salim Durani *saab*.' The same daily published an editorial the next day—a rare thing

---

[165] Vijayakar, Pradeep, 'Salim Durani: Films Are Okay but Cricket Ambition Stays', *Sportsweek*, 22 July 1973.
[166] *The Indian Express*, Delhi edition, 3 April 2023.

for a sportsperson—headlined 'Cricket's Pied Piper' with the intro, 'Salim Durani's career was made of moments that got imprinted on the mind and hearts.'

It went on, 'Numbers are unimportant when a career such as Salim Durani's is up for review [...] Durani was the Pied Piper who could bring the crowds into the stadium [...] It was as the people's champion, though that Durani will be remembered [...] He possessed a fandom well before social media bred cults of armies and team "fams". Everybody loved Salim Durani [...]'

I wrote in his obituary for the UK magazine *The Cricketer*, 'Durani never had a harsh word for anyone and was loved by one and all. They surely broke the mould after he was born.'[167]

All this only goes to show what a remarkable cricketer and person he was, someone who had a special place in the hearts of Indian cricket fans the vast majority of whom would have been too young to have seen him in action. Our hero may even have been part of a famous novel, though indirectly. Vikram Seth's *A Suitable Boy* features a character named Kabir Durani. He plays cricket and is handsome to boot.

But let the last word be with the man himself:

'My career has been glorious for myself and hopefully for the spectators too. My opportunities were limited. I spent five years in the wilderness, then later two years again. These were the best years of my life. But there are no regrets that I have.'[168]

Amen!

---

[167]Ezekiel, Gulu, *The Cricketer*, May 2023.
[168]Memon, Ayaz, 'Mr Sixer!', *Cricketer Asia*, July 1983; in answer to the question: 'What are your thoughts now that your playing days are over?'

Acknowledgements

I would like to express my gratitude to the following people for their valuable contributions to this book.

- Rajender Amarnath
- Abbas Ali Baig
- Vaneisa Baksh
- Bishan Singh Bedi
- Raj Bhat
- Aditya Bhushan
- Theo Braganza
- Nikhil Bhattacharya
- Trinanjan Chakraborty
- Martin Chandler
- Craig Cozier
- Charles Davis
- Dharmenderr Chaudhary
- Rahul De Cunha
- Fredun De Vitre
- Naresh Dudani
- Janelle Duke
- Kailash Gattani
- Stephen Goold
- Neeran Karnik
- Nasser Khan
- David Kaye
- Hemant Kenkre

- Sooraj Kumar
- Marcus Lee
- Boria Majumdar
- Amrit Mathur
- Mushtaq Mohammad
- Ian Subhash Mohan
- Clayton Murzello
- Scott Oliver
- Dr Chandrakant Patankar
- Pat Pocock
- Megan Ponsford
- Rajdeep Sardesai
- Rameshwar Singh
- B. Sreeram
- Vincent Sunder
- K. Martin Tebay
- Karishma Upadhyay
- Sunil Valson
- Anita Agarwal
- Sandeep Dwivedi
- Tushar Trivedi
- Vanita Kumari Singh

APPENDIX

Salim Durani Career Statistics
(by Dharmenderr Chaudhary)

Test Record (Match by Match)

Match	Versus	Date	Venue	Batting	Bowling
1.	Australia	01/01/60	Bombay	18, DNB	0/9
2.	England	11/11/60	Bombay	71, 0	1/91, 2/28
3.	England	01/12/61	Kanpur	37, DNB	1/36, 1/139
4.	England	13/12/61	Delhi	18, DNB	0/38
5.	England	30/12/61	Calcutta	43, 0	5/47, 3/66
6.	England	10/01/62	Madras (NS)	21, 9	6/105, 4/72
7.	West Indies	16/02/62	Port of Spain	56, 7	4/82
8.	West Indies	07/03/62	Kingston	17, 0	2/173
9.	West Indies	23/03/62	Barbados	48*, 5	2/123
10.	West Indies	04/04/62	Port of Spain	12, 104	1/54, 3/64
11.	West Indies	13/04/62	Kingston	6, 4	2/56, 3/48
12.	England	10/01/64	Madras (NS)	8, 3	3/97, 0/64
13.	England	21/01/64	Bombay	90, 3	3/59, 1/35
14.	England	29/01/64	Calcutta	8, 25	2/59, 1/15
15.	England	08/02/64	Delhi	16, DNB	1/93
16.	England	15/02/64	Kanpur	16, 61*	0/49
17.	Australia	02/10/64	Madras (NS)	5, 10	2/68, 1/102

Match	Versus	Date	Venue	Batting	Bowling
18.	Australia	10/10/64	Bombay	12, 31	1/78, 0/48
19.	Australia	17/10/64	Calcutta	12, DNB	6/73, 0/59
20.	New Zealand	27/02/65	Madras (NS)	34, DNB	3/53, 0/4
21.	New Zealand	05/03/65	Calcutta	20, 23	0/49, 2/34
22.	New Zealand	12/03/65	Bombay	4, 6	2/26, 2/16
23.	West Indies	13/12/66	Bombay	55, 17	1/83, 0/42
24.	West Indies	18/02/71	Kingston	13, DNB	0/42
25.	West Indies	06/03/71	Port of Spain	9, 0	2/21
26.	West Indies	19/03/71	Bourda	2, DNB	1/51, 0/47
27.	England	30/12/73	Calcutta	4, 53	0/14
28.	England	12/01/73	Madras (CS)	38, 38	1/24
29.	England	06/02/73	Bombay	73, 37	0/21

NS: Nehru Stadium; CS: Chepauk Stadium (All Bombay Tests played at Brabourne Stadium)

Test Record

Batting
Matches: 29; Innings: 50; NO: 2; Runs: 1,202; Average: 25.04; Highest: 104, 100/50–1/7; Catches: 14

Bowling
Balls: 6,446, Maidens: 317; Runs: 2,657; Wickets: 75; Average: 35.42; Economy: 2.47; S.R.: 85.94; BBI: 6/73; BBM: 10/177, 5/10; wickets: 3/1

Test Centuries
104 versus West Indies–Port of Spain –1961/62

Five Wickets in an Innings in Test Matches
6–73 versus Australia – Calcutta – 1964/65
6–105 (10–177 in the Match) versus England – Madras – 1961
625–47 versus England – Calcutta – 1961/62

First Class Centuries (14)

Score	Team	Versus	Venue	Date
137*	Rajasthan	Vidarbha	Nagpur	30/01/59
131	Indians	Jamaica	Kingston	05/02/71
124	Rajasthan	MCC	Jaipur	22/11/61
120	Rajasthan	Vidarbha	Nagpur	19/11/66
119	Central Zone	West Zone	Bombay	13/02/65
118	Rajasthan	Bombay	Bombay	20/03/64
114	Rajasthan	Uttar Pradesh	Jaipur	23/12/72
110	Central Zone	West Zone	Baroda	13/10/61
109*	Ranji XI	Board President XI	Jamnagar	10/09/72
108	Saurashtra	Gujarat	Ahmedabad	28/11/53
105	Rest of India	Bombay	Calcutta	19/12/70
104	India	West Indies	Portof Spain	04/04/62
104	Rajasthan	Madhya Pradesh	Jaipur	18/12/65
100	Rajasthan	Madhya Pradesh	Udaipur	09/11/63

Five Wickets Hauls in First Class Cricket (21)

Figures	Team	Versus	Venue	Date
8-99	Rajasthan	Bombay	Udaipur	08/03/61
7-46	Rajasthan	Madhya Pradesh	Jaipur	28/12/73
6-32	Indian Starlet	State Bank of India	Hyderabad	21/10/66
6-44	Central Zone	West Zone	Bangalore	11/03/72

Figures	Team	Versus	Venue	Date
6-45	Vazir Sultan XI	Mafatlal XI	Hyderabad	28/09/70
6-48	Rajasthan	Uttar Pradesh	Agra	29/01/72
6-55	Rajasthan	Vidarbha	Nagpur	30/11/70
6-55	Ranji XI	Board President XI	Jamnagar	10/09/72
6-65	Central Zone	South Zone	Hyderabad	25/02/72
6-73	India	Australia	Calcutta	17/10/64
6-105	India	England	Madras	10/01/62
5-20	Rajasthan	Uttar Pradesh	Varanasi	11/11/60
5-26	Rajasthan	Vidarbha	Udaipur	23/11/63
5-37	Rajasthan	Vidarbha	Nagpur	22/11/60
5-42	Rajasthan	Uttar Pradesh	Ajmer	11/12/70
5-47	India	England	Calcutta	30/12/61
5-79	Rajasthan	Vidarbha	Nagpur	10/01/65
5-80	Rajasthan	Uttar Pradesh	Bikaner	26/11/76
5-102	Rajasthan	Mysore	Bangalore	17/03/72
5-120	Central Zone	South Zone	Madras	25/12/65
5-129	Rajasthan	Madhya Pradesh	Jodhpur	22/01/72

Century and Five Wickets in an Innings
109* and 6–55 for Ranji XI versus Board President's XI— Jamnagar—1972/73

Ten Wickets in a First Class Match (2)
10/177 versus England at Madras – 1960/61 and 10/84 versus Madhya Pradesh (1973)

Unofficial Test
Versus Ceylon (1964/65) – Did not bat, Bowling – 1/68

First Class Record

Batting

Matches: 170; Innings: 275; NO: 19; Runs: 8,545; Average: 33.37; Highest: 137*; 100/50 –14/45; Catches/stumps: 144/4

Bowling

Balls: 28,905; Maidens: 1,272; Runs: 12,630; Wickets: 484; Average: 26.09; Economy: 2.62; SR: 59.72; BBI: 8/99; BBM: 10/84, 5/10; wickets: 21/2

Ranji Trophy (for Saurashtra, Gujarat and Rajasthan)

Batting

Matches: 71; Innings: 112; NO: 8; Runs: 3,617; Average: 34.77; Highest: 137*, 100/50 –7/20

Bowling

Balls: 11,576; Maidens: 534; Runs: 4,793; Wickets: 241; Average: 19.88; Economy: 2.48; SR: 48.03; BBI: 8/99; BBM: 10/84, 5/10; wickets: 12/1

Ranji Trophy Record for Saurashtra

Scored 108 and 41 runs, and didn't pick up any wicket in the only match.

Ranji Trophy Record for Gujarat

Matches: 03; Innings: 05; Runs: 199; Average: 66.33; Highest: 74* 100/50–0/2 and 1 wicket @ 30.

Ranji Trophy Record for Rajasthan

Matches: 67; Innings: 105; Runs: 3,269; Average: 33.02; Highest: 137*; 100/50 – 6/18 and 240 wickets @ 19.62.

Duleep Trophy (for Central Zone)

Batting
Matches: 23; Innings: 35; NO: 2; Runs: 1,380; Average: 41.81; Highest: 119, 100/50–2/8

Bowling
Balls: 4,227; Maidens: 191; Runs: 1,945; Wickets: 66; Average: 29.46; Economy: 2.76; SR: 64.04; BBI: 6/44; BBM: 9/87, 5/10, wickets: 3/0

Irani Trophy (for Rest of India)
Versus Bombay (1965/66) – 49* and 0/23
Versus Bombay (1970/71) – 105 and 0/68, 0/19

On Tour with India
1961/62 West Indies Tour: (7 Matches) – 330 Runs @ 25.38, Highest – 104, 25 wickets @ 28.64
1970/71 West Indies Tour (10 Matches) – 402 runs @ 26.80, Highest – 131, 13 wickets @ 41.92

List A Record (Deodhar Trophy for Central Zone)
Versus South Zone (1973/74) – 21 runs and 2/23
Versus West Zone (1974/75) – 13 runs and 2/29
Versus North Zone (1976/77) – Did not bat / bowl.

Index

Aakhri Din Pehli Raat, 156
Abdullah, MJ, 7
Adhikari, Col Hemu, 94, 119
Afghanistan, ix, 1, 3, 4, 5, 109
Afghan lineage, 109
Ahmed, Younis, 155
Akram, Wasim, 49
Ali, Mubarak, 18, 20
Ali, Mushtaq, 140
Ali, Syed Wazir, 22
Allen, David, 66
All-India Cooch Behar Schools Tournament, 25
Al Maktoum stadium, 155
Amarnath, Lala, 25, 40, 41, 45, 148, 149
Amarnath, Mohinder, 155
Amarnath, Rajendar, 41, 149
Amiss, Dennis, 143
Amrohi, Kamal, 156
Anand, Dev, ix, xii, xvii, 156
Anjuman, 26, 28, 29
Anjuman-E-Islam High School, 26
Apte, Madhav, 61, 73
Arnold, Geoff, 142
Ashes, 15, 40, 85, 86
A Suitable Boy, 164

Aussies, 14, 16, 43, 44, 47, 86, 104
Australia, xvii, 8, 9, 10, 13, 14, 15, 16, 17, 35, 40, 42, 46, 47, 54, 56, 68, 85, 86, 87, 92, 94, 97, 98, 102, 103, 104, 105, 110, 111, 112, 115, 131, 139, 167, 168, 169, 170
Australian Board of Control for International Cricket, 14
Aziz, Abdul, 5, 6, 14, 16, 17, 18

Babi, Parveen, 110, 149, 156, 157
Bahadur, Nripendra Narayan Bhup, 26
Baig, Abbas Ali, xvii, 46, 134, 165
Bai Kabibai High School, 28
Banerjee, Shute, 18, 20
Bangalore, xviii, 4, 90, 102, 135, 153, 169, 170
Barbados, 73, 76, 131, 167
Barnes, Sydney, 9
Barrington, Ken, 65, 72
BCCI, 3, 4, 6, 12, 13, 32, 33, 34, 37, 50, 51, 53, 63, 68, 79, 92, 95, 100, 117, 118, 119, 120, 134, 144, 151, 159
BCCP, 23
Bedi, Anju, 157

Bedi, Bishan Singh, 79, 96, 97, 98, 101, 104, 123, 127, 145, 146, 153, 155, 157, 165
Benaud, Richie, 39, 40, 43, 44, 46, 85, 92
benefit matches, 159
Benjamin, Sunil, 107, 108
Bhagwat Singh of Mewar, 31, 108
Bhandari, Prakash, 3, 103
Bhopal royal family, 110
Bhupal Nobles' College ground, 60
Binny, Roger, 161
Board of Control for Cricket in Pakistan, 23
Bobjee, C.N., 36
Bolton Cricket League, 52
Bombay Combined Schools, 26, 27
Borde, Chandu, 42, 44, 50, 62, 93
Brabourne Stadium, 43, 44, 45, 65, 82, 84, 132, 146, 168
Bradman, Don, xvi
Bridgetown, 76, 131
British Empire, 9
Brittain-Jones, Jack, 7, 14
Brown, Alan, 66
Bukhatir, Sheikh Abdul Rahman, 158

Calcutta, xv, xviii, 5, 6, 17, 23, 44, 47, 62, 68, 69, 79, 86, 87, 88, 92, 94, 95, 96, 97, 99, 118, 119, 140, 141, 143, 144, 153, 167, 168, 169, 170
Camacho, Steve, 126
captaincy, 13, 53, 57, 60, 72, 73, 111, 113, 121
Caribbean tour, 78
Cave, Harry, 30
C.B. Rubie's XI, 8
Central India, 7
Central Lancashire League, 52
Central Zone, 38, 55, 56, 58, 64, 87, 91, 104, 120, 132, 134, 138, 140, 143, 147, 151, 152, 153, 159, 169, 170, 172
Ceylon, 8, 85, 170
Chaman Bhai ki Medhi, 2
Chandrashekhar, B.S., 79, 84, 88, 90, 91, 96, 132, 150
Chappell, Ian, xvii, 110
Chari, S.V.T., 17
Charitra, 150, 156, 157
Chauhan, Chetan, 143
Chowringhee, xv
Churchill, Winston, 1
Civil Disobedience movement, 13
C.K. Nayudu Lifetime Achievement Award, 3, 159
Close, Brian, 65
Colah, Sorabji, 18
Commerce College Ground, 29
Commonwealth XI, 78
Contractor, Nari, 26, 46, 69, 70, 72, 73, 76, 109
Covid, 163
Cowdrey, Colin, 65
Cozier, Tony, 128, 130, 165
Cricket Association of Bengal, 96
Cricket Australia, 14

Cricket's Pied Piper, xvi, 163

Davidson, Alan, 41, 42, 43, 46
Delhi Tournament, 6, 8
de Mello, A.S., 7, 12, 13
Desai, Vinayak, 30
Destiny's Child, vii, xv, xviii, 39,
   68, 116, 128
de Villiers, AB, 49
Dev, Kapil, xvi, 109
Dexter, Ted, x, 65
Digvijaysinhji, 2, 14, 21
disciplinary committee, 67
Doordarshan, 97, 161
Dossa, Anandji, 5
Dowe, Uton, 121
Dubai, 155
Duleep, 12, 35, 63, 64, 85, 87, 91,
   102, 104, 120, 132, 134, 147,
   172
Duleepsinhji, K.S., 12
Duleep Trophy, 63, 64, 85, 87, 91,
   102, 104, 120, 132, 134, 147,
   172
Dungarpur, Raj Singh, 33, 34,
   81, 90
Durani Trophy, 135

economy rate, 98
Eden Gardens, xv, 27, 69, 94, 120,
   141
Engineer, Farokh, xvii, 70, 72,
   120, 141, 145, 155
England, x, xvii, xviii, 7, 8, 9, 11,
   12, 13, 14, 15, 17, 18, 20, 23,
   35, 39, 40, 43, 46, 48, 49, 51,
   52, 54, 56, 61, 64, 65, 66, 69,
   71, 72, 78, 83, 84, 85, 87, 92,
   94, 99, 102, 105, 109, 112, 115,
   120, 121, 131, 132, 135, 139,
   140, 141, 142, 143, 145, 146,
   148, 151, 152, 153, 155, 167,
   168, 169, 170

Feroze Shah Kotla, 153
film, x, xii, 141, 156, 157
Foster, Maurice, 121
Fry, C.B., 9

Gaekwad, D.K., 40, 62
Gandhi, Indira, 92
Gandhi, Mohandas Karamchand,
   10, 13
Gandotra, Ashok, 3, 105
Ganges, 33
Gattani, Kailash, 81, 107, 108,
   134, 136, 137, 145, 159, 165
Gatting, Mike, 126
Gavaskar, Sunil, 5, 28, 106, 107,
   114, 115, 121, 122, 124, 127,
   130, 131, 135, 136, 141, 142,
   158, 159
Ghalib, Mirza, 106
Ghose, A.N., 118
Ghosh, J.D., 152
Ghosh, S.K., 134
Gifford, Norman, 143, 145
Gill, Lall Singh, 3
Giridhar, S., 127, 151
Goddard, Trevor, 53, 98
Gopaldas, MA, 7
Gopinath, C.D., 59, 62, 117
Government of India, 48
Grace, W.G., 9

Great Chell, 52, 53
Greig, Tony, 139, 141, 143
Gucht, Paul van der, 20
Guha, A.K., 134
Guha, Ramachandra, xvi, 108, 156
Guntur, 159
Gupte, Subhash, 33, 42, 58, 73
Gymkhana Club, 100

Hall, Wes, 37, 48, 50, 53, 73, 121
Hardikar, Manohar, 61
Haridwar, 33
Harvey, Neil, 42
Headingley, 51
Hindlekar, Dattaram, 17
Hobbs, Jack, 8
Holder, Vanburn, 122
Hunte, Conrad, 50, 73, 75, 93
Hussain, Dilawar, 17

Ideal High School, 28
Illingworth, 139, 143
Imperial Hotel, 67
Independence, 10, 12, 21, 65, 83
Indian Cricket, 5, 26, 29, 32, 36, 37, 63, 64, 74, 83, 86
Indian Express, xvi, 163
India XI, 39, 104, 108
Indore, 32, 38, 140, 143
Indravijaysinhji, R.K., 29
IPL, x, 13, 49, 50, 113, 162, 163
Irani Cup, 79, 91, 95, 102, 104, 120
Irani, Zal, 79, 118

Jadeja, Ajay, 163

Jaffer, Wasim, 28
Jaipur, 2, 3, 61, 62, 66, 81, 90, 104, 150, 153, 169
Jaisimha, M.L., xvi, xvii, 76, 95, 112, 118, 128, 129, 134, 135
Jamnagar, ix, xi, 2, 18, 21, 22, 26, 27, 29, 78, 139, 160, 163, 169, 170
Jardine, Douglas, 8, 110
Jeoomal, Naoomal, 7
Jessop, Gilbert, 9
Jinnah, Mohammed Ali, 23
Jones, Dean, 49
Joshi, C.G. 'Chandu', 107, 108

Kabul, ix, 1, 2, 3, 4, 6, 109
Kambli, Vinod, 28, 48
Kanhai, Rohan, 73, 74, 75, 77, 78, 124
Kanpur, 38, 40, 41, 43, 47, 48, 56, 66, 84, 86, 104, 111, 141, 144, 161, 167
Karachi, ix, 1, 2, 3, 6, 8, 9, 14, 16, 21, 22, 23
Kathiawari, ix, 10
Kenny, Ramnath, 46
Khan, Ain Rashid, 6
Khan, Iftikhar Ali, 21, 35, 110
Khan, Imran, 6, 155
Pataudi, Mansur Ali Khan 'Tiger', xvii, 21, 35, 70, 72, 73, 75, 76, 81, 83, 88, 93, 97, 101, 104, 108, 109, 110, 111, 112, 113, 114, 115, 116, 117, 120, 134, 135, 143, 161, 163
Khan, Mohammed Yusuf, 156
Khyber Pass, ix, 3, 4

Kingston, Jamaica, 75, 77, 121, 122, 124, 128, 167, 168, 169
Kiwi, 30, 87
Knott, Alan, 139
Kumar, Dilip, 156
Kumari, Meena, 156
Kumble, Anil, 42
Kunderan, Budhi, xvii, 45, 47
Kutubuddin, 29

Lake Pichola, 34
Lal Bahadur Shastri stadium, 134
Lancashire League, 48, 50, 51, 52
Lawry, Bill, 86, 104, 143
Laxman, V.V.S., 48
Lewis, Desmond, 121
Lindwall, Ray, 46
Lloyd, Clive, x, 93, 97, 101, 125, 126, 127, 128, 131
Lord Harris Shield tournament, 26
Lord's, 7, 12, 15, 17, 51, 77, 139, 151

Macartney, Charlie, 15, 16, 17, 18, 33
Madras' Corporation Stadium, 65
Maharaja of Cooch Behar, 25
Maharaja of Patiala, Bhupinder Singh, 11
Maharajkumar of Vizianagaram's XI, 8
Maharana of Udaipur, 31
Manjrekar, Sanjay, 28
Manjrekar, Vijay, 33, 58, 90

Mankad, Vinoo, xvi, 2, 18, 19, 20, 25, 27, 31, 32, 36, 38, 48, 51, 52, 56, 57, 58, 59, 60, 68, 69, 77, 78, 98, 99, 106, 109
Mansoor, 35
Marshall, Nariman, 2, 18, 61
Marylebone Cricket Club, xviii
Mathur, L.N., 63
Mayo College, 107
May, Peter, 65
MCC, xviii, 65, 145, 169
McDonald, Colin, 42
McMorris, Easton, 121
Meckiff, Ian, 42, 46
Megan Ponsford, 15, 166
Meherhomji, Khershed, 17
Mehra, Vijay, 76
Melbourne, 9, 14
Memon, Ayaz, 114, 160
Menon, Suresh, xvi, 79
Merchant, Vijay, 19, 28, 60, 95, 105, 117, 118, 144
Mid-Day, 1
Mid-Wicket Tales, 3, 56, 151
Mobed, Minocher, 7, 17
Mohammed, Hanif, 22, 56, 91
Mohammad, Mushtaq 22, 56, 57, 140, 166
Moin-ud-Dowlah Gold Cup tournament, 80, 85, 120
Mr Sixer, xvii, 25, 153
Mukherjee, Sujit, 48, 98, 99
Mukherji, Raju, 20, 26
Munwani, Harish, 24, 25, 142
Murzello, Clayton, 1, 166

Nadkarni, Bapu, 60, 61, 62, 64,

70, 84, 85, 86, 87, 88, 96, 97,
  98, 99, 102, 103, 113
Nagarwala, ND, 44
Narayan, Jagaddipendra, 26
National Defence Academy, 27,
  28
National Films Division, 141
National Institute of Sports, 61
Navle, Janardan G., 7
Nayudu, C.K., 3, 7, 18, 36, 39,
  51, 159
Nayudu, C.S., 36, 39
NDA, 27
New South Wales, 103
New Zealand, 30, 43, 54, 62, 85,
  87, 94, 102, 103, 104, 112, 146,
  168
North Staffordshire, 52
Nurse, Seymour, 50

O'Neill, Norman, 42, 86

Padma Shri, 48
Pai, Ajit, 105
Pakistan, 4, 5, 21, 22, 23, 28, 40,
  42, 43, 54, 56, 65, 69, 91, 132,
  155, 158
Pakistan Cricket Association,
  28
Pal, Suvam, 3, 6
Panchkuian Road, 148
Parffit, Peter, 70
Partition, 12, 21, 28
Patankar, Chandrakant, 62, 166
Pataudi royal family, 21, 109
Patel, Jasu, 29, 40, 41, 44, 68
Patel, J.M. Framjee, 11

Pathan, 4, 6, 99, 156
Patiala, Bhupinder Singh, 11,
  13, 14
Pentangular tournament, 7, 13
Pepper, Cec, 52
Phadkar, Dattu, 48, 118
Pied Piper, xvi, 163, 164
Pocock, Pat, 140, 144, 145, 146,
  155, 166
Port of Spain, x, 74, 76, 84, 124,
  128, 129, 130, 131, 167, 168
Prabhakar, Manoj, 48
Prabhu, K.N., 74, 126, 128, 135
Pradyumansinhji,
  Manoharsinhji, 30
Prasanna, E.A.S., 70, 72, 78, 79,
  90, 91, 96, 98, 114, 115, 118,
  123, 124, 125, 128, 129, 133,
  134, 140, 149, 150
Press Club, 162
Prime Minister's Office, 144

Queen's Park Oval, 75, 76, 124

Raees, 22
Raghunath, V.J., 56, 127, 151
Rajamani, R.C., 3
Rajan, Sunder, 131, 145, 152
Rajasthan Cricket Association
  (RCA), 34
Rajasthan Patrika, 4
Raja, Wasim, 155
Rajkot, 2, 26, 30, 33, 37, 78
Ramaswami, N.S., 5, 32, 36, 37
Ramchand, G.S., 32, 40, 109
Ramji, L., 2, 12
Ranji Trophy, 2, 6, 8, 9, 14, 18,

19, 20, 22, 25, 26, 27, 28, 30,
31, 32, 33, 35, 36, 48, 55, 56,
57, 58, 60, 61, 62, 63, 73, 80,
82, 83, 85, 91, 96, 102, 103, 107,
120, 132, 133, 134, 138, 147,
159, 171
Ranjitsinhji, 9, 10, 12
Rao, U. Prabhakar, 58
Ray, Dutta, 94, 95, 96, 116, 117, 118, 119
Rege, Milind, 136
Rekha, 80, 160
Rest of India, 8, 55, 91, 102, 104, 120, 169, 172
Rhodes, Wilfred, 9
Richardson, Peter, 70
Richardson, Vic, 110
Richards, Viv, 49
Rodrigues, Mario, 10
Roshanara Club ground, 6
Roy, Ambar, 105
Roy, Pankaj, 46
Roy, Sitesh, 100
Russia, 1
Rungta, Kishan, 34, 57, 58, 59, 60, 108
Rutnagur, Dicky, 60, 82, 128
Ryder, Jack, 5, 14, 15

Sadiq, 22
Saheb, Jam, 2, 9, 14, 18, 19, 20, 21
Saldanha, Nicky, 137
Santa Cruz airport, 132
Sarbadhikary, Berry, 78, 79, 128
Sardesai, Dilip, ix, 118, 123
Sardesai, Sopan, 27, 31, 38
Sarin, Gautam, 157

Saurashtra, ix, 2, 21, 25, 26, 27, 29, 30, 31, 43, 78, 157, 169, 171
Saurashtra Combined Schools, 26
Seth, Vikram, 164
Sharadashram Vidyamandir (English), 28
Sharjah, 158
Sharma, Parthasarthi 'Parath', 107, 108, 135
Shastri, Ravi, 28, 99
Shaw, Prithvi, 28
Sheffield Shield, 37, 103
Shillingford, Grayson, 122
Shivalkar, Padmakar, 137, 145
Shukla, Rakesh, 154
Sidney Poitier, xvii
Sind, 6, 7, 8, 9, 16, 17, 19, 21, 22, 23, 28, 33
Sind Madrassah-tul-Islam, 23
Singh, A.G. Kripal, 40, 59, 67
Singh, Arjun, 34
Singh, Hanumant, 35, 102, 108, 150
Singh, L. Amar, 2, 8, 12, 18, 19, 20, 48
Singh, Laxman, 108
Singh, Rabindra 'Robin', 3
Singh, Rameshwar, 2, 4, 5, 45, 94, 95, 166
Singh, Suryaveer, 59, 81, 108, 137, 140
Smith, M.J.K. (Mike), 83
Smith, Steve, 49
Sobers, Garry, x, 37, 48, 49, 50, 52, 67, 73, 92, 93, 97, 101, 112, 113, 121, 122, 124, 125, 126,

127, 128, 129, 130, 131
Sobers, Gerry, 52
Solkar, 99, 121, 123, 124, 136, 137, 138
Sood, Man Mohan, 45
South Africa, 15, 40, 54, 98, 162
South Cheshire League, 52
South Zone, 102, 133, 134, 151, 170, 172
Special General Meeting, 119
Sporting Union club, 96
Sport & Pastime, 72, 88
Sportstar, 1, 72
Sportsweek, 75, 95, 133, 134, 135, 140, 144, 149, 150, 158, 162, 163
Sri Lanka, 65, 85
Statham, Brian, 65
Stevens, Gavin, 42, 46
Stockport, 52, 53
St Xavier's (Fort), 28
Sunderam, G.R., 81, 90, 108
Sunder, Vincent, 137, 166
Sunny Days, 114, 122, 130, 159
Sutcliffe, Herbert, 8

Tagore, Sharmila, xvii, 109
Tarapore, Keki, 119
Tarrant, Frank, 14
Tata's industrial house, 11
Ted Dexter, x, 65
Ted Dexter's, x
Tendulkar, Sachin, 28, 56, 151
Test match, xv, xviii, 4, 9, 14, 20, 37, 42, 44, 50, 56, 62, 73, 80, 93, 131, 139, 147, 156, 163
Thakore Saheb of Rajkot, 26, 30, 37

The Cricketers Benefit Fund Series, 158
The Hindu, 3, 16, 18, 43, 44, 72, 79
The Illustrated Weekly of India, xviii, 57, 114
The Indian Cricket Field Annual, 82, 83
The Instrument of Accession, 21
The Statesman, 28, 69, 71, 75, 105
The Times of India, 11, 27, 41, 66, 74, 126, 135, 158
The United Nations, 21
The Victory Story, 141
Time, 88, 156
Trueman, Fred, 51, 65
Trumper, Victor, xvi, 9
Twitter, 1

Udaipur, 31, 34, 60, 169, 170
Udaipur Palace, 34
Umrigar, Polly, 42, 60, 61, 62, 70, 72, 74, 75, 76, 77
Underwood, Derek, 139, 142, 144, 145
Union Government, 99
Universities Grants Commission (UGC), 101
University of West Indies, 101

Vazir Sultan Tobacco XI, 120
Vengsarkar, Dilip, 28
Venugopal, C.N., 41
Viceroy of India, 13
Victorian England, 9
Vidarbha, 38, 58, 81, 147, 169, 170
Vijayakar, Pradeep, 157, 162, 163

Viswanath, G., 1, 2, 29, 30, 127
Vishwanath, G.R.,121, 127, 129, 134, 152, 153, 160, 163, 168, 169
Vizzy, 8, 13, 14

Warne, Shane, 68, 126
Watson, Chester, 50
Wazir (brother of Hanif), 22
Wensley, Albert, 19, 20
Western India States, 8
West Indies, ix, x, xi, xv, 37, 40, 42, 49, 50, 53, 54, 56, 67, 72, 74, 75, 76, 77, 78, 79, 92, 93, 95, 100, 101, 114, 117, 119, 120, 121, 123, 124, 128, 131, 132, 135, 152, 153, 159, 161, 167, 168, 169, 172
West Zone league, 9, 31
Wilde, Simon, 10
Willingdon, Lord, 13, 14, 67
Wisden Asia Cricket, 13, 112, 154
Wisden Cricketers' Almanack, 65
World Cricketers: A Biographical Dictionary, 89
Worrell, Frank, 48, 49, 53, 67, 73, 74, 75, 77, 78, 92, 100, 101

Yadvendrasinhji, R.K., 19
Yeshwant ground, 32

www.ingramcontent.com/pod-product-compliance
Lightning Source LLC
Chambersburg PA
CBHW020231170426
43201CB00007B/392